THE DEVIL CAN'T COOK
Spaghetti

THE DEVIL CAN'T COOK
Spaghetti

USING

Faith

TO

OVERCOME

Fear

MICHAEL ESSANY

HiddenSpring

Cover art: © Hugo Chang, istockphoto.com
Cover design by TG Design
Book design by Lynn Else

Library of Congress Cataloging-in-Publication Data

Essany, Michael, 1982–
    The Devil can't cook spaghetti : using faith to overcome fear / Michael Essany.
        p. cm.
    ISBN 978-1-58768-049-6 (alk. paper)
    1. Fear—Religious aspects—Christianity. 2. Essany, Michael, 1982–
3. Faith. I. Title.
    BV4637.E88 2009
    248.8′6—dc22

                                                        2008042371

Published by HiddenSpring
An imprint of Paulist Press
997 Macarthur Boulevard
Mahwah, New Jersey 07430

www.hiddenspringbooks.com

Printed and bound in the
United States of America

Contents

Contents

For Christa

Introduction

In World War II, during the Nazi's relentless daylight raids over much of Great Britain, a small sign was found posted above the entrance to a severely damaged church along the English countryside. It read: "When fear knocks, it shall be faith that answers."

Whenever I think of this sign, I'm reminded of a great many people throughout history who have demonstrated extraordinary faith in the presence of almost unfathomable terror. Collectively, they embodied a level of faith that most of us, God willing, will never have cause to summon. Yet their example serves as a wonderful reminder of all that can be conquered with the immense power of great faith.

Growing up, I often overheard my grandmother profess to be "worried sick" about something. Usually, her concerns were far more benign than her dramatic commentary might have otherwise suggested. But the very idea of being worried to the point of physical sickness was a concept I understood.

As a little boy, in fact, I suffered from severe upset stomachs. Although our family physician never discovered anything seriously wrong with me, my frequent bellyaches we eventually attributed to normal "childhood anxieties." In other words, I was *literally* worried sick.

Fear, of course, is an inescapable consequence of humanity. It is a core human emotion that affects everyone in varying degrees of strength and frequency. By responding to painful, threatening, or otherwise negative stimulus, fear is an inherent survival mechanism, but one that doesn't strictly abide by its intended biological function.

Most of us, after all, don't experience fear only when our immediate survival is endangered. Instead, fear is an unavoidable daily familiarity. Yet, unlike the myriad diagnosed, and in some cases treatable, phobias that classically center on one perceived tangible threat—heights, water, and so on—the most insidious if not universal apprehension, conversely, stems from the very *lack* of a particular threat. That is, it's the natural uncertainty that accompanies many aspects of life and death that, beyond question, causes the greatest anxiety for individuals of all ages.

As a child, my first known fears were all inextricably connected to the unknown. What would happen to me after I died? Will I ever be forgotten or abandoned by those around me? What was I put on this earth to do? All were unspeakably vital questions that ultimately spoke to the strength of my faith. As a young man I was ravaged by the burdens of bearing what can most accurately be described as an incomplete faith.

Faith, after all, is about more than just believing in God. It's also about expectation. According to the dated analogy, if I lie in a hammock, for example, I have faith that the hammock will not collapse. In other words, my faith extends beyond just knowing that the hammock is there. I also believe—without any ostensible proof—that it will not allow me to fall. Likewise, our faith in God should relate to both his consistent presence in our life and his ability to prevent us from falling. For many of us, however, we simply cannot lie in a hammock without first "proving" that it won't collapse.

Fear, on the other hand, has it much easier. Unlike faith, fear rarely necessitates any proof to compel our expectations. In this regard, the paradox between our faith and our fear is striking. That is, our expectations are far more easily compelled by our fears than they are by our faith, particularly when confronting the unknown.

Arguably, much of our growing concern about the unknown today seems related to a perceived decline in robust faith. While certainly not pleasant to recognize and even more difficult to confront, we as a culture and society have grown unspeakably lazy. And, in many cases, tragically, so has our faith—in ourselves, in each other, and even in God.

Believe it or not, unlike our computers, cell phones, and iPods, the Bible doesn't require new software upgrades to remain functional and relevant. But in a high-tech civilization with a rapidly dwindling attention span, it's easy to see why some folks simply cannot retain faith in any book more substantive than the latest James Patterson novel. So, for many, the Bible has quickly joined the ranks of an arcane and antiquated relic of the past with little or no relevance to contemporary life. And the terrible reality, of course, is that some will never rethink this belief unless the cast from *CSI* forensically proves that God and his teachings remain valid.

Today more than ever, we want, need, and demand proof of everything. Faith alone has become horribly insufficient to allay worries—big or small—about life, death, and everything that fills the gap. As a result, the "seeing is believing" doctrine of our day is swiftly amounting to what could very well become the greatest human tragedy of our time.

When referring to the mounting number of people losing their faith to fear, some prefer to incite the melodramatic phrase "crisis of faith." Personally, however, I don't believe there is a crisis of faith as much as there is a laziness of faith.

Having faith, after all, requires some pretty hard work at times. Yet everywhere we turn there are new modern conveniences, gadgets, and trends poised to make our lives just a little bit easier. From the new TV remote that controls everything except your mother-in-law to the latest cell phone that utilizes more technology than the first Apollo moon shuttle, the overwhelming majority of us want to simplify our lives with simpler solutions, simpler contraptions, and, perhaps most dangerously, simpler beliefs.

To be sure, the Lord our God is many things—Heavenly Father, Giver of life, Forgiver of all sins—but the one thing he *isn't* is simple. And unfortunately for simple human beings like you and me, our faith isn't all that simple either. Fortunately, at least, some of the most effective ways to better understand and apply our faith in daily life *are* quite simple. And I was blessed to learn many of them on my long, often treacherous, but ultimately enlightening journey from living life in fear to eventually welcoming it with faith.

1

My First Fear

I had never seen so many children crying in one place before. Everywhere I turned, there were little boys and girls tearfully pleading with their departing parents for refuge.

"It's their first day of kindergarten too," my mother said, thinking that a reminder of other children's anguish would somehow ease my own. "Before long, you won't even miss me."

Shortly after Mom kissed me goodbye on the weathered concrete steps of St. Bridget's Catholic School, her shrewd prediction actually came true. I loved my mother unconditionally, of course, but on this most harrowing day of my young life so far, the emotional capacity of my five-year-old frame was already fully occupied, with no additional space available for lamenting my mother's temporary absence.

Unlike my peers, who mostly bewailed the common schoolhouse anxieties born of severed parental ties, the whimpers that escaped me on that first day of kindergarten resulted from a different apprehension altogether. For me, the start of school itself prompted few related qualms. My Aunt Lucille's wake, on the other hand, was considerably more unsettling.

As a little boy growing up in the small Midwestern town of Hobart, Indiana, there were few ostensible threats to my well-being. I lived in a reasonably safe neighborhood, on a quiet street, with a loving family, and enjoyed a small, closetless bedroom that never left me wondering what hideous creatures might be dwelling there amidst the darkness of night. If truth be told, there was very little for me to fear as a child—except, that is, for what almost every family member around me openly feared on a surprisingly consistent basis: death.

Before I had even outgrown the choking hazards posed by the majority of my toys, death was already a concept with which I was well acquainted. As a young boy in a large and particularly old Italian family, I routinely experienced the loss of aunts and uncles, many of whom I knew well, and others whom I could barely recognize.

Through it all, my relatives constantly sought to sugarcoat the gravity of death and its subsequent impact. But most of the time I was also privy to their solemn and uncensored conversations in our living room about the pain and suffering that frequently preceded death for family members I had seen sometimes only a few days earlier. The dialogue would often grow so disturbing that I would flee to my bedroom in fear of being the Grim Reaper's next victim in our immediate family.

Woody Allen once observed: "It's not that I'm afraid to die, I just don't want to be there when it happens." By the time I was old enough to realize that I was much too young to worry about death, my epiphany provided little comfort. By now, death was much too close to me and my family to not at least contemplate my eventual and unavoidable demise.

According to many psychologists, there comes a distinct moment in every life when fear first arrives. For me, fear arrived when I first perceived the difference between how my family discussed death with me and how they discussed it among themselves. It seemed a tremendous contradiction for them to speak joyfully in one breath of the promise of everlasting life and then cower at the very notion of death in another.

To be sure, the perceived physical pain attributed to death was not what most petrified my juvenile wits. Instead, it was the concept of hell as presented by virtually everyone around me that thoroughly horrified my mind's eye beyond the capacity for rational thought. Hell, unlike death, held a consistent tone in family conversations. Speaking to me or to each other, the grown-ups in our house never sugarcoated any definition or depiction of a fiery hell. And while all were decent, God-fearing Catholics, they collectively speculated on a habitual basis about which recently departed loved ones may or may not have found their way into God's kingdom. In the process—consciously or not—they would seemingly take turns reflecting in general on their own professed inventory of sins and their ultimate chances for salvation.

Without question, mine was a devout Catholic family whose faith long preceded the first generation to leave the old country and settle in America. With no exceptions, faith came first in our household. But even though our Catholicism was an unwavering source of strength and guidance during great periods of difficulty and even greater loss, my family always seemed to spend more time fearing their faith than celebrating it.

Before long, I too adopted a fear-based approach to faith and began wondering as to which deceased kin would likely see the proverbial light at the end of the tunnel. More selfishly, perhaps, at the ripe old age of five I also began questioning if I was already living a life worthy of eternal salvation. Given my youthful naivete at that time, this was certainly a scary period of contemplation for me. And, unquestionably, it was amplified by my parents' determination that I was now old enough to attend my first wake.

As it turned out, my deceased relative du jour—Aunt Lucille—was scheduled to be shown at the Geisen Funeral Home, coincidentally, on my first day of kindergarten at St. Bridget's.

In light of my father's plan to pick me up from school and drive directly to the funeral home, Mom sent me to kindergarten already dressed in appropriate mourning attire. Wearing a short-sleeve white dress shirt, black slacks, and a grey tie longer than my entire body, I showed up on the first day of school dressed like the Alex P. Keaton of kindergarten.

"Well, aren't you handsome!" proclaimed Mrs. O'Grayla, our sweet kindergarten teacher who, despite her youthful acuity, appeared ripened enough to have been teaching since the Civil War.

My classmates, on the other hand, weren't as easily impressed by my prim and proper appearance. Most, in fact, were inquisitive about the reason for my murky garb.

"My Aunt Lucille died," I repeated frequently throughout the day, reluctant to face an unnerving situation that I had no choice but to face later. "I have to go to her wake tonight."

"Are you going to touch her?" asked a kid named Paul, provoking squeals from the girls and giggles from the boys.

"I don't know," I quickly replied, further nauseated by the newly acquired imagery.

"If you touch her face," continued Paul, "you can tell if she's in hell or not."

"You can?" I asked, confident that Paul was wrong but intrigued nonetheless.

"If her face is hot," he said "that means she's burning in hell."

At first, I didn't exactly know what to make of this audacious kid's apparent knowledge of cadavers and eternal damnation. Initially, I thought Paul was merely trying to act like the tough Italian kid his physical appearance otherwise suggested. Then again, this is the same guy who was crying harder than all the little girls before school that morning.

With time, however, Paul and I grew to become more than just passing classmates. Soon we became good friends. And it wasn't long at all before I realized that Paul and I shared many of the same childhood fears.

On the infrequent occasions I found myself playing at Paul's house, it was difficult to escape the consistent efforts of Paul's overbearing Catholic mother to keep her only son in line. Indeed, she did more than just put the fear of God into him. She also put the fear of hell into him.

Incapable at his young age of grasping the biblical depiction of hell as a tortuous repository for wicked souls, Paul was taught that hell is where life's joys are simply extinguished. So, for Paul, hell was understood to be a place where they didn't serve spaghetti, the singular joy of his young life.

Skillfully exploiting her son's penchant for pasta in order to keep the house quiet, whenever Paul and I carried on like the kids we were, Paul's mother would invariably invoke the sternest warning in her illustrious repertoire: "The devil can't cook spaghetti!"

Like me, Paul was also terrified by the prospect of burning in hell. And although neither of us had a clear idea of how we could ensure a one-way ticket to the pearly gates of heaven, my immediate plan was to at least observe the good deeds—and potential wrongdoings—of those within my own family. With any luck, time would tell which lives provided the best examples for me to follow as I grew into an adult.

Luckily, my Aunt Lucille's wake presented a timely opportunity to begin viewing the world through more spiritually analytical eyes.

Shortly after arriving at the funeral home, which curiously smelled of both death and Parmesan cheese, I found myself the veritable Roger Ebert of Catholics. Clothed in my now wrinkled mourning attire and exhausted from a long day of school and self-inflicted mental torment, I paced the gloomy halls of Geisen's quietly critiquing the words and actions of practically everyone in attendance.

Soon I had compiled a running mental checklist of those who didn't seem to be mourning sufficiently. According to my early estimates, nearly half the room was bound for hell on the basis of their perceived inappropriate behavior.

Failing, however, to take into account that a good Italian family celebrates—and mourns—with massive quantities of Mostoccioli Marinara, I found abhorrent the idea that everyone was going to a local dining hall for dinner after the wake. "Who can eat at a time like this?" I wondered, certain that anyone who filled their plate during a time of bereavement was also destined for the flames of hell. Not long after, though, my irrational powers of perception were turned inward at my own growling stomach. My foolish thought process had alerted me to the erroneous notion that I too was committing a grave and hypocritical sin by craving the very food I had condemned others for wanting to eat.

No matter how hard I tried to make sense of what was or wasn't acceptable behavior in the eyes of God, I always returned to a point of absolute confusion that further frustrated and confounded my almost competitive drive to secure a place in heaven. But I didn't know how to avoid going to hell and I was certain that my uncertainty alone was enough to condemn me. Surely, I thought, a good boy would instinctively know what to do. But hoping to not disappoint my parents and other immediate family members, I concealed my growing unease and bewilderment the best I could.

The facade finally fractured, however, when I first laid eyes on my Aunt Lucille's peaceful but unnaturally painted face. Having never observed a corpse, Aunt Lucille's rosy cheeks didn't strike me as a contrived cosmetic artifice for beautifying a dead body. Instead, I interpreted her reddish complexion as confirmation of Paul's belief that if the face of a dead person is warm she is burning in hell.

As the time drew near to pay our final respects at Aunt Lucille's magnificently adorned casket, I found myself nestled tightly in my father's comforting arms. Together we walked along the dark, worn carpet that displayed an intricate pattern of interweaved lines that seemed to resemble the equally intricate knots that distressed my tentative stomach. As I recall, each step closer to the casket further aggravated my fragile emotional state. By now, my nervous system could no longer deal with such overpowering anxiety. Before we even reached the casket, I informed my father that I wasn't feeling well.

"It's okay," Dad responded. "Your Aunt Lucille would be happy you're here."

But as we finally reached our morose destination, my stomach at last collapsed under the enormous self-imposed stress I had now been enduring for almost a full day. With no advanced warning, my wound-tight little body relinquished its forced composure and I began throwing up all over my dad and on the closed bottom half of Aunt Lucille's flowery casket.

As everyone gasped in horror at my unanticipated and violent physical upheaval, I saw in the overdramatic eyes of those closest to the spectacle the fear that I may be a child in need of an exorcism. Had my mother sent me to school that day with a bowl of split pea soup, I would have likely been doused with holy water before the last remnants of lunch could even leave my quivering mouth.

And as though such circumstances weren't already embarrassing enough, during my awkward emotional breakdown I found myself crying harder than any child had on the steps of St. Bridget earlier that morning. Much like Aunt Lucille's pint-size orange cat, which fled in fear of a ringing door bell, I too proved a scaredy-cat among the captive funeral home audience that was my entire family.

Conventional wisdom holds that nature unhurriedly sculpts who an individual eventually becomes by means of his environment, upbringing, experiences, and choices in life. Incredibly, fear is seldom included on this critical short list of formative dynamics that cumulatively mold an individual into his mature form.

To be sure, who we become in due course is inextricably linked to what we once feared—or still continue to fear. As a kid, my fear of death and, accordingly, the existence of hell, spilled over into many other facets of my youth. For a time, in fact, I grew fearful of almost everything in my path. Without question, fear fundamentally defined—and habitually threatened to derail—my journey from adolescence to adulthood.

Growing up in a melodramatic Italian family that was as close-knit as it was eccentric didn't help at times either. Although my fears eventually grew distinct from those of my family (money, divorce, or the cancellation of a Tony Danza sitcom), I stood to face an enormous whirlwind of anxieties ultimately born of school, friends, puberty, appearance, sex, ambition, and my own overactive imagination.

Fortunately, long before I was old enough to know much of anything else, I already knew that I could not resign myself to living the rest of my life in fear of the world around me and, most importantly, my own religious faith.

Although the years ahead brought with them innumerable fears born of life's uncertainties, my search for sanity and success in a self-imposed world of unrelenting fears ultimately led me down a path of personal growth, spiritual revival, and a renewed outlook on the beauty of existence, the power of God's love, and the often misunderstood role played by fear in one's life.

2

Abandonment

Shortly before two o'clock in the morning, I was abruptly awakened by the emergency lights beaming through the heavy blue curtains of my small bedroom window. Before I could even climb out of bed to investigate the spectacle on our lawn, I was struck by the unfamiliar sound of panicked voices as they reverberated throughout the paper-thin walls of our house and also within the frame of my six-year-old body.

As my bleary eyes were just beginning to focus on the ambulance parked in eerie silence at the end of our driveway, I detected the unmistakable sound of my mother crying. My instincts, of course, naturally drew me to my mother's presence. But my cold, bare feet were ostensibly welded in place before the windowsill. I was not only too scared to move, I was also too curious. Living at home with my parents and grandparents, I could only deduce from the sound of my mother's intense weeping that she *wasn't* the one in need of emergency care.

Through the dimness of night, I observed from my bedroom window a burly police officer open the tattered screen door on our porch to accommodate the rushing paramedics. As I wiped away the tears now streaming down my face, my vision was at first impaired as the stretcher was frantically wheeled from the house. But before the rear doors on the ambulance were slammed shut, the image of my grandmother barely clinging to life beneath an oxygen mask was permanently seared into my young memory.

Just as memorable, perhaps, was how I felt the moment after the ambulance departed with our family vehicle—presumably carrying my mom, dad, and grandpa—trailing exceptionally close behind.

The night my grandmother suffered this massive and almost fatal heart attack I developed an immediate and inordinate fear of being left alone. Before I learned that my father had stayed behind to look after me, I was overcome with an almost paralyzing sense of abandonment. Having already been frightened by the prospect of death, I was now equally petrified by the notion that I would somehow be left behind—either as a result of those around me dying off or because my loved ones would simply forget I was still there.

Throughout the early part of my childhood, my fears often resembled Hollywood celebrities. That is, they never stayed single for long. Whenever one fear emerged, another vaguely connected fear would soon follow to compound the entire situation.

Before I had even acclimated to the general prospect of abandonment, my focus had already shifted to an even more sobering concern. In no time at all, my utmost distress was that I felt alone in the sense that God wasn't with me. As I stood frozen in place at my bedroom window I couldn't help but wonder where God was and why he wasn't with me. Why was I even allowed to feel so terrified in the first place? I had long been familiar with stories of how God comforted others who felt alone. Had I maybe done something to make God not love me anymore? These were all questions I found myself asking as I watched the ambulance pull away.

Looking back, as a little boy, I was *literally* looking for God, as though the moment my grandmother was carted off to the hospital with my family tailgating behind, George Burns would pop out of the closet and tuck me back into bed.

In no time at all, the advent of my fear of abandonment soon turned into the first real spiritual emergency of my life. In my worst moment of isolation, I was baffled by my inability to detect the comforting presence of God.

Of course, my primary concern on that unforgettable night was the well-being of my grandmother. The second was being left alone. But the third, wondering why God had seemingly deserted me, was undeniably the most emotionally unsettling.

Unfortunately, in my naïve youth at the time—and for several more years to follow—I was utterly incapable of observing just how significant and tangible God's presence really was during those terrifying early morning hours of my grandmother's illness.

Years later I heard a poignant story that somewhat reminded me of this early experience.

As the tale goes, there was a man who lived by himself near a river. He heard a news flash on the radio that the town was about to flood. The man refused to move, however, believing that God would not abandon him.

In a matter of hours, the river rose and the man's house began to flood. In no time at all, a rescue worker rowed by in a canoe and shouted for the man inside his flooding house. But the man refused to join the rescue worker. "God will not abandon me," the man said.

A few hours later, the river completely flooded the town. The man took refuge on the roof of his crumbling house. Within minutes, a helicopter swooped down and lowered a rope ladder. Stubborn as ever, the man still refused to leave, believing that God would not abandon him.

Shortly thereafter, the man drowned.

Upon greeting Saint Peter at the gates of heaven, the man angrily insisted on a meeting with God.

"How could you abandon me, Lord?" the man asked. "I've done everything I could think of to please you. Why did you leave me helpless?"

"I sent you a news flash, a rescue worker, and a helicopter," God replied. "What more do you want from me?"

There are many times in life when we simply expect too much, as though the hand of the Almighty will personally descend to pluck us from a perilous fate. It was God, after all, who answered my first prayer by allowing my grandmother to live after suffering a coronary that even her doctors were astonished didn't kill her. What's more, God didn't allow me to be alone. I didn't know it at the time but my father stayed behind to look after me while Mom and Grandpa went to the hospital. The recuperation of my grandmother and the loving care of my father—who, fortuitously, didn't have to work midnights this particular week—were both made possible by God's watchful eye.

For many people caught up in an emotional and stressful experience, it's incredibly easy to feel deserted—by others or even by God. What we commonly don't manage to perceive until hours, days, maybe even years later, are the ways in which God *was* there for us. And no matter how bleak or unsettling circumstances may appear at the time, He is *always* there for us.

It took a very long time before I understood this valuable lesson about God's frequently inconspicuous guardianship of our lives. And for the remainder of my early childhood, I was relegated to live each day with yet another fear tacked on to my growing list of worries that habitually interfered with my ability to enjoy life, find comfort, and look to the future with hope rather than fear.

3

When Angels Bowl

As the legend goes in my family, my grandfather was supposedly struck by lightning as a little boy while standing on the porch during a terrific storm. Incredibly, not only did Grandpa survive unscathed, he also emerged surprisingly unafraid of thunderstorms. Likely the result of my grandfather's tall tale, I never developed the somewhat ordinary childhood fear of weather-related phenomena.

As I recall, one year for Halloween when my parents hosted a party for my friends from school, a powerful thunderstorm coincidentally added to the spooky allure of the festivities. To me, the bright bolts of lightning that ripped through the ominous dark sky were simply awesome. My excitement, though, was soon forced into retreat when one of the kids in attendance began crying intensely.

To my naïve bewilderment, thunderstorms were not as popular with some kids as they were with me. Before long, my parents and I were wholly confronted with a packed living room of panicked children.

Fortunately, there was one other kid also brazenly undaunted by the inclement weather. And together we tried calming everybody down. But while I employed straightforward logic to explain that the storm would soon pass without harming anyone, the other kid opted to share a story that he professed to have learned in Sunday school.

"It isn't *really* a storm outside," he coolly informed the cluster of trembling children. "Thunder means the angels above are bowling." The loud rumblings, he explained, were nothing more than an angel's ball rolling down the alley followed by a strike.

As I stood there with my jaw open listening to a tale taller than even my grandfather's, the kids surprisingly quieted down and accepted the seemingly pleasant idea of angels bowling. My immediate reaction, of course, was relief in that everyone had finally relaxed. My second reaction was the startling realization that I needed smarter friends.

How anyone could actually believe that thunderstorms were really angels bowling befuddled my brain endlessly. Not only was it nearly impossible to consider, I also found the idea enormously unsettling. I didn't want to picture heaven's choir of angels as a bowling league composed of John Goodman look-alikes with feathered wings and a halo.

In my mind, the children at my party had been deceived. But I don't hold the storyteller accountable. The real fault belonged to whoever began perpetuating that outrageous story in the first place.

After the party that evening, I lay awake in bed for hours contemplating how many of my own beliefs may have also been rooted in bald-faced lies. Yet as I prayed for greater understanding, I was quickly reminded of the tremendous no-no it was to doubt the word of the Lord or those imbued with the Holy Spirit to speak on his behalf. As I recalled while tossing and turning like a rotisserie chicken, my friend—the grand storyteller, that is—claimed that the idea of angels bowling had actually originated from Sunday school. If so, I was fearful to question the integrity of the claim, particularly if it had come from a priest.

As a child, I didn't have a mature understanding of the surprisingly beneficial role played by doubt in one's own faith. If truth be told, there comes a point when we all speculate to a degree about some aspects of Christianity that our rational brains won't allow us to accept without initial resistance. However, those struggling to believe, for example, that Jesus walked on water should take solace in knowing that Peter at first did the same. Believing that Jesus had resurrected Lazarus was difficult for Martha to accept. Equally doubtful was Andrew, particularly of Jesus' ability to feed five thousand with only five loaves of bread. And, of course, we all know the story about Thomas. So if even the firsthand witnesses of Jesus' miracles—including his own apostles—occasionally grappled with believing what often seemed unbelievable, is it any wonder that we do the same?

Unfortunately, many of us consider doubt—much like fear—a disgraceful mark of an unripe faith. But, in reality, doubt is enormously favorable to faith in that it ultimately reassures us of our deepest beliefs. Even though I could not see it at the time, God had preemptively answered my prayer for the ability to detect anything that may falsely influence or dilute my beliefs. Strangely enough, I did not recognize the undeniable irony in asking God for the ability to recognize mistruths when the entire ordeal was actually born of my recognizing one! Indeed, God has imbued each of us with both faith and a rational intellect. At times, they square off and remain at odds for as long as we struggle to reconcile what we believe with what we think. But, fortunately for humanity, it is what we believe—our faith—and not our thoughts that matters most to God. Ultimately, we are all saved by our faith, even amidst the storms of doubt that occasionally cloud our sight.

In the garden of Gethsemane, even Jesus exhibited fear in his prayers. He expressed doubt in the present time of uncertainty, but faith in God's ultimate plan. In this regard, Jesus' example is an important one for those besieged by balancing doubt with faith. Certainly, it is natural or "normal" to doubt what we do not know for sure. But what is unknown to us is not unknown to God. According to Saint Augustine, "Faith is to believe what you do not yet see; the reward for this faith is to see what you believe."

As a child, however, all I could see was the ever-widening contingent of people eager to believe the dumbest things imaginable so long as it satisfied their doubts in the moment. Consequently, I grew enormously distrustful of anything and everything that sounded contrived just for the sake of easing minds. And as a likely result, it became increasingly difficult to relieve my own worries as I worked diligently to guard against potentially tampered relief. Even though it would take many more years to finally realize that prayer itself provides sufficient relief from all the fear and doubt anyone could possibly have, for the time being, I proceeded with life afraid to ask the "big questions," wary of false beliefs, and completely unable to reconcile my doubts with my faith.

By now, whether or not the angels were really bowling in heaven was entirely irrelevant. All I knew for certain was that I had consistently bowled gutter balls with my faith here on earth.

4

The Saving Grace
of Humor

For the first two years of my life, few things captivated my imagination like the utility drawer in our funky 1970s kitchen. Conveniently positioned between a stove antiquated by log cabin standards and a refrigerator that hummed louder than a Harley Davidson, this sacred repository for kitchen utensils never failed to excite and entice my juvenile wits.

Before I was old enough to know much else, I knew that the scissors my mother used to pierce the cellophane wrapper of my favorite cookies were stored in *that* drawer.

Day after day, the slightly rusty shears with a worn crimson grip provided a reliable after-dinner portal to dessert bliss. And although I wasn't allowed to use them, or any other scissors, without parental supervision, the thought of having unfettered access to this important tool was much too tempting a notion for my cookie-craving tummy to ignore.

Inevitably, somewhere amidst the terrible twos, this compelling temptation finally provoked action.

In the temporary absence of my mother's watchful eye, I swiftly capitalized on the open utility drawer by stealthily seizing those long-sought-after scissors. And before my mother's maternal radar could detect my furtive handiwork, I had put the scissors to use on practically everything.

From cutting the strings off my sweatshirt to shredding the cover of the phone book, I wasted very little time with this treasured new toy. Before long, in fact, my versatile cutting tool made its way to the telephone cord. My grandparents, after all, had a cordless. Why shouldn't I?

Alas, my cutting spree spanned only a few minutes. Yet significant "alterations" had been made throughout the entire kitchen. Within moments, however, Mom had returned from retrieving the laundry and I was shamelessly caught red-handed.

Of course, by this particular point in my young life I had not yet witnessed the unadulterated wrath of an irate Italian mother. But as my mom's incensed eyes penetrated my admittedly artificial expression of innocence, it was then that I first experienced a legitimate fear of my very own mother.

"What have you done?" Mom asked as the laundry basket fell from her white-knuckle grip.

"Nothing," I responded while slowly backing into the hallway.

Mumbling inaudibly as she picked up the severed telephone cord from the kitchen floor, my mother was fuming in total disbelief.

"I think I'm going to be sick," she said, wiping the sweat from her brow.

"Don't get sick, Mommy," I replied, having recently been taught how to dial 911. "I won't be able to call for help!"

In an instant, my mother's barely contained anger had turned into uncontainable laughter.

As it turned out, my unintentionally ironic quip had gotten me off the hook. And, as a result, by the tender age of two, I had learned more than just a simple lesson about the appropriate use of scissors. I also learned the saving grace of humor.

Over time, humor would become a most reliable weapon for counteracting the multitude of fears that plagued my youth. By the time I finished kindergarten, fear had become a major part of my life. But for me, humor provided both a means for coping with fear and a way to convince those around me that I wasn't as afraid of life, death, and just about everything else in between as I probably was.

Fortunately, I was never discouraged from using humor in any situation, even as it pertained to the church. Although my family might have been too religiously conservative to condone any church humor, I was comforted and encouraged by the stellar sense of humor of one of the finest men I have ever known.

To this day, in fact, I can't pass a single library shelf without hoping for a wistful moment in vain that a book about the life of Father Stanley Milewski rests somewhere among the sea of titles.

The narrative of Stanley Milewski's extraordinary eighty-four years is certainly more than a biography of one Catholic priest. His life and humor, in effect, are forever intertwined with the lives of those who learned from his deep faith and gained from his spiritual guidance.

Most of my family attended Father Stanley's parish, Holy Family Catholic Church, in Gary, Indiana. As lifelong parishioners, they became close, dear friends with Father Stanley, not to mention great admirers of his wisdom and humor. Eventually, this bond between my family and Father Stanley would be passed down to me—and probably sooner than anyone expected.

As a child, there were few occasions that I looked forward to as much as Sunday morning mass—specifically, it's conclusion. I still maintain that church made me one of the earliest known victims of Restless Leg Syndrome. Without fail, every service gave rise to my mother having to steady my impatient leg from noisily tapping on the church's exposed concrete floor. Invariably, this was the scene week after week, as dismissal could never come soon enough for me.

My fidgety peers in adjacent pews recurrently appeared to share a similar eagerness. But while they were probably just excited to go home, my impatience was rooted in the thrill of my family's post-service ritual of spending the rest of the morning with Father Stanley.

Over the years I was exceptionally fortunate to hear Father Stanley tell many stories while visiting our home. But, when primarily addressing me, Father Stanley spoke most about the importance of serving God in all aspects of one's life.

I still vividly recall the awkward unease that gripped my stomach the first time he asked me what I wanted to be when I grew up. In the past, I never liked answering this question. Time and time again, no matter how thoughtful an answer I supplied, I always felt I was somehow dissatisfying those who had inquired. And, after a while, I not only began to fear this monumental question, I also grew concerned that I would never find my true calling in service to God.

Many within my family hoped that I would become a priest, doctor, or any other occupation that significantly helps others in a tangible way. Regrettably, I never felt "called" by such a pursuit. And, for that very reason, I never expressed interest in one. My reluctance to become a priest, though, was not something I readily shared with others.

But the first time Father Stanley asked what I wanted to be when I grew up, I struggled to answer honestly while trying to avoid dashing anyone's grandiose hopes for my destiny—especially Father Stanley's.

Thinking on my feet and seeking to reconcile the incomplete pieces of my knowledge of the life of Christ, I simply informed Father Stanley of one possible option for my future.

"I want to be a pilot," I said.

"A pilot?" Father Stanley inquired with wide eyes.

"Yes," I replied. "I want to be a pilot…just like Jesus."

During the long pause from Father Stanley that followed, I confidently reclined back in my chair thinking that I had not only impressed this wise man of the cloth but had also discovered a career that actually excited me.

At this point in my young life, however, I was possessed of the incorrect and altogether absurd assumption that Pontius Pilate was a nickname for Jesus. Apparently, I must have been under the ridiculous impression that *Pontius* was some sort of Israeli airline for which Jesus was a pilot between working miracles and providing eternal salvation.

As I recall, after his lengthy digestion of my outrageous comment, it was all that Father Stanley could do not to spurt his tea across the living room. Even though I was much too young at this point to realize the hilarity of my innocent gaffe, Father Stanley's tremendous sense of humor was sincerely tickled by the reasoning behind my wanting to become a pilot.

"Well, you can be whatever you want to be in life," said Father Stanley, "just use the gifts God gave you to carry out his plan for you."

As a child, I was perpetually befuddled by the concept of "God's plan" for me. What's more, I was totally oblivious to the "gifts" I was purportedly given. To my knowledge, lip-syncing to my grandfather's Dean Martin albums could potentially be classified as a talent, but just how useful it could be to humanity was a different story altogether.

My sudden professional quandary immediately led me to reflect on those in my family, our community, and even on television who seemed to possess an amazing sense of mission in life; the folks who inoculate babies in Africa or save rain forests in Brazil. These individuals, it appeared, were blessed with an ability to hear a faint, divine voice that points exactly to where God needs them to go. As a result, they find their calling, their passion, and the very core of their existence.

Even before the last of my baby teeth had fallen out, I developed the third most profound fear of my youth—never finding my life's purpose.

As Father Stanley once put it, "We're all drafted to a great calling. Some just never hear their number."

Although my previous apprehensions about death and abandonment were significant in my formative years, I was now equally petrified by the thought of not hearing my calling and, consequently, failing to serve God.

But just as I had erred before and certainly would again, I botched yet another golden opportunity to recognize that the answers I sought had actually been in front of me all along.

Per usual, I was bound for another roundabout journey to discover that humor had more to do with my calling than just to help me cope with the fear of never discovering it.

5

The Odyssey

A singular joy from childhood commonly took place on Sunday mornings at an eatery called *The Odyssey*. On most weekends after Sunday mass, my parents and I—along with Grandma and Grandpa—would share a late breakfast or early lunch at our favorite diner. Conveniently enough, the Odyssey was located almost exactly halfway between our house in Hobart and our parish, Holy Family Catholic Church, in Gary, Indiana.

I can still vividly recall the appetizing smell of freshly baked crepes, buttery milk pancakes, and humongous cinnamon rolls that nearly rivaled the size of my juvenile cranium. Invariably, though, my typical menu selection was more predictable than the varying array of enticing dishes available. For me, a cheese omelet hit the spot almost every week. And for as long as we continued this Sunday ritual, I rarely strayed from this particular culinary delight.

Week after week, hefty pots of coffee and good conversation were the staples at our booth. In some ways, in fact, those memorable visits to the Odyssey provided another form of Sunday school education. Quietly sitting there and listening to my parents and grandparents talk about life, share stories, and debate topical issues probably did more for my early maturation than anything else during those formative years.

To be sure, there was never a shortage of frivolous banter either. Almost habitually, Dad and Grandpa would deliberate the relative merits of an old movie they stayed up late to watch the previous evening. At times, it seemed that James Cagney was as much a fixture at our table as my cheese omelet. In retrospect, I can't recall my mom or Grandma ever laughing as much as they did when Dad and Grandpa exchanged Cagney impersonations. Strangely enough, though, I spent more time watching Mom and Grandma's uproarious reactions than the Rich Little wannabes.

Once, when I was about three years old, my family and I were joined at the Odyssey by Father Stanley. Around this time I started to believe that my family had chartered their own priest. I could think of no other explanation for how much time my parents and grandparents spent with him. Nonetheless, I loved Father Stanley and treasured every moment in his presence.

I still recall our meal that Sunday morning in lucid detail. More specifically even, I recall the prayer in which Father Stanley led my family before devouring the picturesque dishes that had just been placed upon our respective settings.

As Father Stanley made the sign of the cross at the prayer's conclusion, his right hand inadvertently whacked his glass of orange juice. In one of those surreal moments where everything transpires in slow motion, the waves of Father Stanley's spilling beverage traveled across our table and thoroughly marinated my cheese omelet.

Before anyone spoke a word, I looked up and directly into Father Stanley's eyes. The moment he returned the gaze, I said without any hesitation: "You dirty rat!"

Everyone reacted as though it was the funniest thing they had ever heard in their lives. In hindsight, I suppose a three-year-old impersonating James Cagney by telling a Catholic priest that he's a dirty rat *is* rather funny.

Father Stanley, as I remember, bellowed for the whole restaurant to hear. Yet I still remember the look upon the face of a noticeably uptight, staunchly conservative woman in the opposite booth. She was an older lady whom I recognized as a parishioner at our church. Apparently she had overheard my comment to Father Stanley. Judging by her countenance, she had concluded that my young life was already damned straight to hell. At that point, though, I didn't care. I mean, I got a laugh—and a big one at that.

In retrospect, the Odyssey was not only a favorite restaurant from my youth; to an extent, the title itself—the Odyssey—served as an appropriate metaphor in some ways for my childhood. Incredibly, almost every time I saw Father Stanley I somehow managed to make him laugh, even before I was old enough to understand how. Eventually, my penchant for humor and his consistent urging for me to answer my calling would inspire me to follow what would soon become a unique odyssey both of fear and of faith.

6

The Big World
Out There

During those long summer nights of the late 1980s, my parents were less than strict when it came to enforcing a bedtime.

On most evenings I elected to stay up late and watch television with Grandpa. Of course, I did almost everything with Grandpa. I clung to him incessantly. Whenever we watched television, for example, I would lie on the ground, stomach down, so that the tips of my little toes rested on the top of Grandpa's feet as he sat in the recliner behind me.

One time, during a commercial, I glanced over my shoulder only to find a pair of empty slippers. This was Grandpa's first—and only, I might add—successful evasionary tactic. He never escaped unnoticed again.

When we weren't watching television, Grandpa and I usually amused ourselves with a host of other activities, often at the expense of my grandmother's sanity. But one time, when I was about six, I stayed up long after my parents had retired just to watch a program everyone always discussed but I had never seen—the *Tonight Show*.

Understandably, I was much too young to comprehend the topical jokes at that time, yet I was instantly mesmerized by the show. I mean, there he was—Johnny Carson, a comedic giant larger than anything my miniscule brain was capable of grasping. This was nearly two decades before high-definition broadcasting was pioneered, but at that particular moment, the picture I saw was clearer than any other. The silver-haired King of Late Night was laughing it up with another show business legend, Bill Cosby. It was a scene that instantly inspired visions of the fun Grandpa and I would probably have in conversation once I had grown up.

As a little boy, humor was obviously very important to me. From helping allay the severity of my deepest fears to enabling me to connect with my older relatives, humor was an equalizer. With hindsight, it's easy to understand why Johnny Carson was so appealing to me. He didn't appear ravaged by anxiety or exhibit any difficulties communicating with a wide variety of eclectic guests. In short, Carson was everything I wanted to be but wasn't: relaxed, confident, and able to make the world a slightly happier place.

With time, however, I began reflecting on Father Stanley's repeated counsel. On many occasions, in fact, I was encouraged to listen carefully to my heart, one of many avenues through which God communicates his wishes, or our calling, to us. Of course, if every kid's calling was the first occupation that caught his attention, this would likely suggest God wants a lot more astronauts, rock stars, and baseball players in our world. But youthful imaginations are allowed to soar for a reason. And, occasionally, a dream that takes root in childhood remains through adolescence. Only then can the foolish fancies of youth be separated from the sober intentions of the heart. In my case, however, I didn't wait for others to take me seriously. I knew after watching Johnny Carson for the very first time what my calling had been all along.

Unfortunately, apart from my uncle's Elvis impersonation, no one in my family had any experience in show business. The entertainment industry, to be sure, was as far removed from me, my family, and our community as any other industry imaginable.

Northwest Indiana, to put it mildly, had never been a nucleus for top entertainment. And for this reason, many tried to scare me into believing that my dream could never be realized if only because I was from the humble state of Indiana.

Life in the Hoosier state was always presented to me as somewhat of a temporary deployment. "It's a process," people said. You grow up here and then flee the first chance you get, like finding an escape hatch in the dungeon.

Growing up, I never understood why so many people spoke unfavorably of Indiana. For some folks, spending more time in our state than you absolutely had to was equivalent to wearing braces after your teeth are straightened. Why suffer needlessly?

My exposure to this line of thinking began during kindergarten, where a petite lady with curly brown hair and fuzzy pastel sweaters used to assist our teacher. She often spoke wistfully of "the big world out there," always, I thought, with a twinge of palpable bitterness about her own inability to experience it. To this woman, variety was the spice of life, and Indiana was little more than a bowl of leftover tuna.

The early part of my childhood was spent in Hobart, a quiet Hoosier town of about twenty-five thousand. It was a charming place to live, just not terribly exciting. I mean, "What happens in Hobart stays in Hobart" was never on the drawing board for a city slogan. But those first years in Hobart were among the happiest of my life.

My parents and I lived upstairs in my grandparents' modest little dwelling on LaSalle Street, only a few miles outside of Lake George. As a little boy, I thought John Mellencamp's music video for "Little Pink Houses" was actually filmed in our neck of the woods. My neighborhood was practically identical to the community depicted in one part of the song's video. When I heard that Mellencamp was from Indiana it seemed likely that Hobart was indeed the subject of "Little Pink Houses."

When I wasn't busy incorrectly determining which rock stars were singing about our block, I was usually involved in all the activity common around our house back then. As an Italian family, there was always good reason to celebrate, eat, invite company, eat, drink some wine, and then eat again. On most days, though, the extent of our excitement was limited to a visit from Uncle Tony and Aunt Esther.

As a child, there were few things I enjoyed more than listening to my uncle's World War II stories. In 1943 Uncle Tony was among the Marines fighting to secure Tarawa in the Gilbert Islands. Nearly one thousand of the five thousand Marines who invaded were killed on the beachhead. Two thousand more, including Uncle Tony, were severely wounded. Even though I must have seen Uncle Tony's Purple Heart a thousand times, my excitement never waned each time he brought it over.

Because he and my aunt lived only a few houses down on the same side of the street, they would actually drop in quite frequently, usually for afternoon coffee with my grandparents in our finished basement.

As far as I could tell, my mom, a music teacher, and dad, a steel worker, were also content during our days in Hobart. By all accounts, the upbringing they provided for me was very much a traditional Midwestern one.

As a little boy, though, Hobart represented practically all that I knew of the outside world. My real introduction to "the big world out there" would eventually come from the mid-sized Zenith television that rested heavily in its monolithic console on the red shag carpeting of our family room. This television, it seemed, was always on. And every beauty and blemish of the planet was steadily on display for my little eyes to absorb. Thankfully, I had plenty of grown-ups around to explain some of the scary content—mostly from newscasts—that would regularly catch my attention.

Looking back, one of my first observations of television was that Indiana never really came up. I suppose it didn't help that we lived in northwest Indiana and received the Chicago newscasts. To me, though, it simply appeared that there was no news in Indiana worth reporting.

Although my family appeared generally pleased with our geographic lot in life, the occasional criticism would be vocalized. One of the first barbs I ever heard came from my uncle. His comment was directed toward a state law prohibiting liquor stores from also selling milk. To this day, I can't tell you if such a law is really on the books. Personally, I haven't encountered many shoppers who purchase fine liquor where they also select their dairy products. Then again, maybe Cap'n Crunch has more in common with Captain Morgan than I realize.

Whenever Indiana was discussed—or disparaged—at home, it usually had to do with jobs. My father, who spent his entire adult life in the brutal conditions of a functioning steel mill, wanted me to get a good education and soar to unparalleled heights. Dad worried that Indiana lagged behind in some aspects and wouldn't be able to accommodate new industries and the promising careers they beget. He largely agreed with the message ingrained during kindergarten that there weren't many big-break opportunities around.

Needless to say, when people eventually began linking my chances for success to "the inopportunity of Indiana," I certainly didn't know any better. All I knew was that show business sounded terrifically exciting. And despite some who saw my curious infatuation with late-night comedy as a passing—and highly unusual—childhood phase, my fascination with the genre continued throughout adolescence.

In the summer of 1991, my family and I bid farewell to Hobart but not to Indiana. In fact, we relocated to the nearby city of Valparaiso—or "Valpo" as the locals call it. For several years my parents had been building a home in a fairly new subdivision called Shorewood Forrest. Apart from our new address, though, life in Valparaiso was largely the same as life before. My grandparents even sold their old house and moved in with us. Thankfully, I liked our new home and, more importantly, our new hometown.

Valparaiso, which means "Vale of Paradise," had been a favorite place of mine to visit while living in Hobart. My parents and I would typically head to Valpo on the first Saturday after Labor Day to attend the Popcorn Festival. This annual celebration, which attracts thousands of spectators, features a parade, entertainment, great food, local music, and a variety of interesting vendors and personalities. The festival is held in honor of popcorn guru and Valparaiso native, Orville Redenbacher. Orville himself even participated in most of the parades until he passed away in 1995.

Since the Popcorn Festival's inception in 1979, Kathy Butterfield, the wife of Valparaiso Mayor David Butterfield, has organized and hosted the annual Popcorn Festival Talent Show. Dozens of amateur singers, dancers, musicians, and comedians from all across the community would participate without fail in this traditional staple of the event's festivities.

For as long as I had been attending the talent shows, they were held in the beautiful one-thousand-seat auditorium at Valparaiso High School. Every year, hundreds of ticket-paying spectators filled the seats and provided heartfelt support to the many local contestants. It certainly wasn't *American Idol*, but the typical judges were far from slackers. Actually, it wasn't uncommon for there to be three or more judges with stellar resumes in all facets of the performing arts.

By the time I entered sixth grade I was seriously considering filling out the little application to perform in the talent show. Indeed, my childhood fondness for comedy had not diminished the least bit. I was saddened, of course, by Carson's retirement in 1992, but somewhere deep in the impractical bowels of my overactive imagination, I believed there might be a place for a guy like me in television one day—Hoosier and all. And maybe—just maybe—winning the Popcorn Festival Talent Show would be a first step.

Accordingly, one afternoon in late spring of 1995, I called my dad at work and kindly asked him to pick up an application for the talent show on his way home from work. As I recall, that very evening after dinner, I sat in my room meticulously pouring over the form like it was a great work by Shakespeare. I must have stared at the actual date and time of the competition for fifteen minutes. To be honest, I was afraid; scared to death, actually. I mean, I had foolishly fantasized about my calling to become an entertainer since I was practically old enough to formulate any fantasy at all. In that particular moment, however, it finally hit me—self-doubt. I had never considered, not even for a split second, if I had enough talent to do what I wanted to do.

Before turning in that night, I ripped up the application. As a kid who first feared death, abandonment, and then never finding my true calling, I had now grown fearful of even myself.

7

Butch

Before I could even recognize the likes of Big Bird, Kermit the Frog, or even Cookie Monster himself, as a child, I was first acquainted with three well-known characters of a different sort: Leonid Brezhnev, Yuri Andropov, and Konstantin Chernenko.

Almost every morning at breakfast I bore witness to my grandparents' passionate conversations about the issues of the day. Like clockwork, Cold War politics were always discussed, either in historical reference or modern relevance.

Understandably, at that time, I possessed not even a partial understanding of what "those Soviets" were up to in their part of the world. All I knew unequivocally was that my grandparents were afraid of them. Even in the dwindling days of the US-Soviet geopolitical rivalry, my grandparents still feared the likelihood of nuclear war as though the thirteen days from October 1962 were going to be replayed.

One of my earliest memories from childhood, in fact, is lying at my grandfather's feet in our family room watching a rebroadcast of the epic 1983 made-for-television movie called *The Day After*. Starring Jason Robards, *The Day After* offered an explicit and unsettling presentation of the effects of a nuclear holocaust on the local residents of Lawrence, Kansas.

According to my grandfather, the devastating impact of a real thermonuclear war would far surpass the horrendous depiction of death and destruction portrayed in the movie. I didn't understand why at first, but Grandpa spoke to me about the dangers of nuclear war as though I would ultimately have some say in preventing it. With time, however, it became clear that my grandfather was merely communicating how the threat of global nuclear conflagration would be passed on to my generation.

But the true lesson I learned from my grandfather's routine admonitions about World War III had nothing, in fact, to do with a nuclear holocaust. What my grandfather's anxiety actually conveyed was the practical utility of fear in a society—to control people.

The policy of MAD, or Mutual Assured Destruction, for example, effectively managed to keep both Soviets and Americans from getting too uppity with each other for more than one-half century. There's nothing quite like fear— either real or invented—to keep someone else in line. For my grandparents, not to mention hundreds of millions of Americans and Soviets, the fear of nuclear war likely did more than anything else to effectively prevent it.

For me, on the other hand, as a kid growing up on LaSalle Street in Hobart, our crotchety old neighbor George brought this exact same lesson about fear to light. For the first seven or eight summers of my life, there were many nights I went to sleep petrified by the spine-chilling image of George's vicious dog. So vivid and lifelike were my visions of this satanic animal that I often believed I could hear the beast growling beneath my bed. I wasn't sure if other kids in the neighborhood had similar nightmares about George's dog, but I certainly knew they were aware of this creature's dreaded presence.

As children, a favorite pastime was gathering a bunch of buddies on my front yard and seeing how far our Louisville

Sluggers could launch a pitched Wiffle ball. Although we never so much as uprooted a single blade of grass, our cantankerous old neighbor across the street—whose yard frequently served as the landing pad for our Wiffle ball—would immediately take to his porch whenever we began playing.

"If you kids don't stop," he would shout, "I'm gonna let Butch out!"

As little boys with imaginations run amuck, we recoiled in horror at the thought of Butch rushing out of our neighbor's portentous detached garage and methodically chewing our faces off. None of us had ever actually seen this feared canine, but the stern, graphic warnings were more than sufficient to disperse our otherwise harmless summertime play.

Not until the summer of 1995, four years after moving away from the old neighborhood, did I learn from another former neighbor that Butch didn't really exist. Apparently, this invented watchdog had been used on neighborhood kids for more than four decades. I was merely among the most recent fools to actually fall for it.

Whether it's a nation armed with nukes or a grumpy old man terrorizing children, everywhere you turn there are individuals, religious leaders, politicians, and people from all walks of life in between using fear to somehow influence or control others.

For me, identifying the utility of fear for its practitioners was among my greatest discoveries on the path to freeing myself of the fears that dominated my youth. It was a process, in fact, that began with a personal challenge.

As far as I could tell, fear can only control those who allow themselves to be controlled. For years the fear of Butch had kept me indoors on many occasions where I could have more fully enjoyed a beautiful summer afternoon.

Looking back, I grew angry—more at myself than with my neighbor—for having allowed an artificial threat to impact my youth and now insult my intelligence. What's more, at this point in time, I simply couldn't help but wonder if I was now allowing myself to be controlled by another fear—the prospect of failure in the pursuit of my dream.

It's been said that fear, in its positive capacity, can drive our ambition, keep us sharp and alert to the competition, and be used to silence our critics with stunning success. When viewed in this light, fear is a far greater ally than enemy, but only for those capable of controlling its power.

As a kid inspired to achieve goals that simply could not be attained without a confident and an utterly fearless warlike mentality, I knew I had to demand more of myself and my spirit than I had ever demanded before. But I knew I couldn't do it alone.

Over time, I began praying for the courage to exact more of myself in the pursuit of my dream. I prayed for the strength to face my apprehensions and the ability to sense an opportunity that would be ripe for an inaugural test-drive of the fortitude I had to summon sooner or later.

As it turned out, however, the opportunity I prayed for would actually befall me much sooner rather than later.

8

The Top Ten List

Several weeks after I decided to skip out on the summer's biggest—and only—local talent show, I found myself one morning cheerlessly crawling out of bed for a late breakfast of apple cinnamon oatmeal and burnt waffles.

As I sat at our small kitchen table enjoying my dubiously nutritious meal, I noticed my mother half-interestedly watching *Live with Regis and Kathie Lee* on our occasionally color 1982 Zenith television set.

Like my mom, I wasn't really paying much attention to the program, until about five minutes into the opening host chat when the topic of discussion turned to the upcoming ten-year anniversary of the daytime duo's popular morning talk show.

According to a self-deprecating Regis Philbin, no one really seemed to care about the milestone anniversary. And for the rest of the program this humorous sentiment was the popular running joke.

Having seen Regis multiple times on the *Late Show with David Letterman*, I assumed that Dave would likely present one of his legendary "Top Ten Lists" about the anniversary. But the more I thought about it, the more I became inspired to beat Letterman to the punch. I hadn't even finished breakfast before deciding to pen my very own top ten list to commemorate Regis and Kathie Lee's big day.

At the end of the show, I scoured the closing credits for a mailing address to the studio. At that time, the public was encouraged to send postcards and letters as a form of viewer feedback. Luckily, I found the address and headed to my room considerably more cheerful than I had left it only one hour earlier.

Ninety minutes later, I had produced the first comedy material of my "career." My finished product was titled "The Top Ten Reasons Regis and Kathie Lee Are Still Together after Ten Years."

First thing the following morning, I mailed my labor of comedic love with a prayer to the New York studio. I'm still not exactly sure what I was hoping to gain from my list. Naturally, I didn't expect Regis to read my work and then call Letterman to get me a job. If anything, I suppose I just wanted to make whoever opened my mail—a lowly staffer or Regis Philbin himself—laugh out loud.

No more than two weeks after remitting my debut work, I found myself eating breakfast—likely oatmeal and waffles again—in the same seat where I first cooked up the idea for a top ten list. Like before, *Live with Regis and Kathie Lee* was on television. Perhaps neither my mother nor I would have looked up at the screen if not for the following words Regis spoke: "Some young man who is only twelve-years old wanted to help us celebrate our ten-year anniversary."

My mother screamed.

As I sprung from the kitchen counter to hit the record button on our fifty-pound 1990 VCR, Regis began reading my top ten list on live national television. In that very surreal instance, I looked at my mom, who was now crying, to verify that I wasn't suffering a hallucination.

Indeed, it was a weird and yet wonderful turn of events. I was too afraid to enter the Popcorn Festival Talent

Show but now my material was being presented to millions of viewers on live national television. Best of all, to my utter elation, the studio audience responded with waves of genuine laughter.

Afterward, my legs were so weak that I found it difficult to stand. Yet for the rest of the day, I found it even more difficult to sit. Those five incredible minutes from *Live with Regis and Kathie Lee* had inspired me to an unfathomable extent. As soon as the audience had finished laughing, in fact, I could only think of ways to begin making them laugh again.

On many occasions throughout the following weeks and months, I began frequenting our local public library for reasons completely unrelated to school projects. Before long, in fact, my primary impetus for visiting the facility was to research a wide variety of articles, how-to guides, autobiographies—essentially anything that could provide much-needed insight on how an unknown twelve year old from Indiana could break into the television industry.

Needless to say, very few resources available spoke directly to my unique predicament. Nonetheless, one summer afternoon while deeply entrenched in the stacks, I stumbled across what was called *The Autograph Collector's Complete Guide to Celebrity Mailing Addresses*. Even though I was in the market for advice and not autographs, this handy guide contained thousands of current mailing addresses to network television studios, production companies, celebrity fan clubs, and so on.

In a sudden rush of youthful conceit, I approached the checkout counter and forked over a tattered library card from my Velcro wallet with the swagger of a real estate tycoon whipping out his platinum Visa after a business dinner. And, within hours, a massive letter-writing campaign was headquartered in my bedroom.

All in all, before my thirteenth birthday, I drafted more than one thousand handwritten letters to every entertainer working, retired, or unemployed.

Remarkably, less than one month after my first batch of letters had been postmarked, I started receiving a variety of cards and packages, in response. Before long, in fact, I was receiving more mail than my parents.

Once, when our mail was inadvertently delivered to the wrong box, our neighbor, Andy, stopped by to personally return our huge stack of deliveries.

I'll never forget the image of Andy standing on our doorstep talking to my dad.

"You have some impressive pen pals," said Andy to my dad. "It looks like you got a postcard from Betty White."

"Actually," my dad replied, "that's probably for my son."

The note from Betty White, in truth, was among the most personal I would receive.

"Keep your eye on the prize," she wrote, "and the prize will keep its eye on you."

Betty White, however, was not the first celebrity to reply. The speediest response belonged to none other than Mr. Bob Hope.

Incredibly, Mr. Hope sent a brief note kindly wishing me well in the pursuit of my dream. He also attached a beautiful signed photograph, which has been on prominent display on the living room mantle ever since.

Perhaps most incredibly, one evening while my folks were washing the dishes after dinner and I was busy studying, the phone rang. My mom reacted quickest and was first to pick up.

"Hello...Yes...Who's calling?" She asked.

After a lengthy pause, Mom looked blankly at me. Because it wasn't my birthday and I didn't have many friends, I was surprised to learn the call was for me.

"Who is it, Mom?" I asked.

"Joey Bishop," she replied.

Having grown up in an Italian household, my grand-father always played Frank Sinatra and Dean Martin records in the basement at night when everyone else in the house was trying to sleep. By the time I was old enough to talk, I knew that Dean, Sammy, Frank, Peter, and Joey were all in the Rat Pack. And regardless of my young age, I had become a fan. Joey Bishop, in fact, was one of the first few entertainers I contacted.

When Mom handed the receiver to me, her eyes conveyed sheer, almost incomprehensible bemusement at what was actually transpiring. My dad, in fact, even broke a dish amid all the excitement.

"Hello, this is Michael," I said.

"Michael, Joey Bishop."

"Oh my goodness, Mr. Bishop, thank you for calling."

"Well, I got your letter. It was very nice of you to write. I don't know how much advice I can give someone your age, but you need to get in front of people. Develop your style. Finding your comedic voice is half the battle. If you're good, you'll be noticed."

Obviously, I greatly valued Mr. Bishop's advice and still recall practically verbatim every ounce of wisdom he imparted during our surprisingly lengthy telephone conversation. His words, above all else, spoke directly to the fearful kid in me that had once ripped up an application to the Popcorn Festival Talent Show. In this regard, Joey Bishop was like a comedic guardian angel assigned to bolster my confidence and nudge me in the right direction.

Before our conversation ended, my mom requested that I tell Mr. Bishop that if we ever visit California we would take him out to lunch. When I relayed the invitation, Mr. Bishop responded: "Tell your mother I'd rather take the cash."

Growing up, I had always heard that celebrities were stuck-up, self-interested egomaniacs who couldn't care less for the "little people." While I'm sure this is the case for many, my first experience with famous people suggested the exact opposite.

Then in his late seventies, Joey Bishop had not only taken the time to read my letter, he found the number I scrawled on the bottom of the page and actually *called* me. It spoke volumes about the phenomenal person beneath his public persona known for dry, sardonic humor.

Astonishingly, in the weeks that followed my inspirational dialogue with Joey Bishop, more personal letters and replies found my mailbox. They included notes from Jay Leno, David Letterman, Don Rickles, Bob Newhart, and even the King of Late Night himself, Johnny Carson.

In total, my six months of letter writing netted more than four hundred replies. Some, of course, were more personal than others. And while I still appreciated every bit of advice, only one icon of entertainment offered words that truly achieved the stated goal of my efforts—and in one sentence.

Delivered in a plain, unmarked envelope postmarked from Beverly Hills, a note from Milton Berle contained a message that would never leave me: "Good luck, Michael. Just remember...if opportunity doesn't knock, build a door."

The Devil Can't Cook Spaghetti

As an ambitious youngster long fearful that opportunity would never find me, I was promptly stopped in my tracks by the notion of *not* waiting for opportunity to find me. In the months that followed, in fact, "seek and thou shall find" essentially became my guiding principle. And in the summer of 1997, at age fourteen, my quest for exposure and opportunity would unswervingly lead me to a local cable television station in northwest Indiana.

9

A Public Access Miracle

Public access television had always captured my imagination. Both its dismal caliber of programming and questionable function of purpose had perpetually befuddled me. Most public access programs, to be perfectly candid, were a veritable broadcasting train wreck from which I could not turn away.

The first show I ever watched on public access was of a man sleeping. As I recall, he was a fairly robust gentleman wearing only Spider-man boxers and a pair of sleep shades. A home video camera was trained atop a tripod and directed at its subject's peaceful slumber. Occasionally, the sleeping man would roll over, but that was about it. Nonetheless, this program continued to air uninterrupted for one full hour. Looking back, probably the only thing more baffling than this show was that I was actually watching it.

Apart from the "interesting" ideas that some local entertainers would occasionally bring to life on local cable, the station itself also featured the obligatory high school sporting event and regional political talk shows. Our future sheriff, David Lain, even hosted a public access program where he interviewed community notables and discussed local issues. For the most part, though, the programming was bizarre, off-color, and frequently disgusting. The sleeping man, for instance, was followed by a show featuring a guy dressed in a dog suit who pretended to pee on inanimate objects in between reciting old vaudeville jokes.

While the intention behind the creation of public access television is commendable, very few people have used the medium to augment their community's awareness of issues and appreciation of culture.

Essentially, public access television exists as the only form of common-folk media. Due to the 1984 Cable Franchise Policy and Communications Act, all cable companies in the United States are required by law to provide regional airtime to residents through a local cable provider.

The purpose of the legislation was to enrich neighborhoods in the heartland with more original programming pertinent to localized concerns, issues, and values. Consequently, at least one channel through every cable provider is designated—at the cable company's expense—to solely broadcast original programming, known as public access television. Typically, a fully functional television studio is even accessible to the general public at no charge. This is where most of the programs are produced, filmed, and broadcast.

At the end of the day, what it boils down to is that virtually anyone can obtain airtime on public access. It's first come, first serve. The only catch: no advertising. Public access exists purely for local commentary, entertainment, and community awareness. The medium is entirely not for profit. And because there's no money to be made, quality programming is a rare find.

By 1997, it was clear that my future was inextricably linked to public access television. Understandably, I wasn't pleased. But fully aware that no television executive in his rational mind would ever give an untested eighth grader from Indiana his own late night talk show, there was only one avenue available to me for garnering some airtime—public access.

Joey Bishop advised me to get in front of an audience. And Milton Berle suggested I build my own door to opportunity. Perhaps public access, what many viewed as the bottom of the barrel in television programming, would enable me to do both.

So, in early fall, my dad took me to visit the public access station in Hammond, about forty-five minutes west of Valparaiso. The building somewhat resembled the run-down exterior of Mickey's gym in the original *Rocky*.

Dad and I walked tentatively into the Channel 16 studio doors with obvious apprehensions about our environment. There was a receptionist desk in the lobby but, to my surprise, no receptionist. So I grabbed two Tootsie Rolls from the greeting basket and proceeded with my father through the navy blue curtain suspended above the threshold to the studio.

But before Dad and I could fully absorb and appreciate the minutiae of our surroundings, Rob, the public access coordinator and station manager, entered the studio with warm greetings. We had spoken briefly on the phone a few weeks earlier, and I found him to be just as helpful and pleasant in person.

Rob gave us a cursory tour and, before long, he had to break away to address a tape-deck malfunction. As my dad and I sat unoccupied for a few minutes in the edit bay, we noticed a guy splicing together his show on a nearby editing deck. I didn't notice his show as much as his inclination to consistently pick his nose while producing the footage. For a moment, I second-guessed the whole public access idea when I realized that I may have to touch the same equipment this guy was using.

When Rob returned, he asked me *exactly* what I had in mind for a show.

"It's going to be a talk show," I said. "Sort of like the *Tonight Show*."

"Okay," Rob replied. "And what are you going to do on the show?"

"I'm going to interview people and tell jokes. There might even be a sketch or two."

At that particular moment, the nose-picker opted to join our conversation.

"A talk show?" he asked with inquisitive disdain. "Isn't there an age requirement for that, Rob?"

Rob didn't respond to the question. I think he could tell that I was put off by the nose-picker's condescending tone.

"You will need to produce three episodes before we give you a time slot," Rob explained. "If the footage is acceptable, you'll be on the air within a week or two."

Because I was underage, my dad had to sign the requisite papers assuming liability for any potential damages to the Channel 16 facilities. Until I turned eighteen, I had to be accompanied by a legal guardian at all times in the studio.

With a few cursory signatures from Dad, I was now only steps away from my own show—at least in theory.

Although I was itching to be on television like nothing else, I didn't want to go on the air without a quality program. And it would certainly take time to build the show of my dreams, a show that would blow everyone away, especially the smug nose-picker.

Somewhere in my heady imagination, I envisioned a public access talk show that would rival network late night television. It would be a show, I dreamed, that attracted Hollywood's biggest stars and a perpetual national spotlight.

For cable television in northwest Indiana, my vision was a bit unrealistic. After all, public access remained bleak and uninspiring despite my grand visions of potential refurbishment. And with the exception of only a few well-known success stories, public access had primarily swallowed whole the dreams of countless aspiring entertainers who couldn't ultimately rise above this lowly level of community programming. But maybe—just maybe—if I could pull off a public access miracle, I would be well on my way to living my dream and serving what I had come to believe was my life's true calling and purpose.

Unbeknownst to me, however, I was about to encounter a level of profound rejection with the potential to forever instill in me a fear of failure unlike anything else I had previously experienced.

10

Charging Through the Shadows

As a little boy, one of my favorite and most mischievous activities was surprising my grandparents late at night by jolting out of bed and running straight into their room without prior warning. Time after time, I would catch them off guard by enthusiastically jumping on their bed and giving both yet another hug and kiss goodnight.

Thankfully, Grandma and Grandpa had long welcomed these unannounced visits from their three-year-old grandson and reciprocated with tons of affection only grandparents can offer.

Unfortunately, though, their bedroom door wasn't open *every* night. And, over time, my parents lost count of the number of times they were awakened by the startling sound of their child crying in the hallway after painfully colliding head first with the bedroom door.

Through it all it never occurred to me that I should probably slow down when turning the corner that led into my grandparents' room. Instead, I just charged through the shadows, full steam ahead.

As Father Stanley would teasingly observe, perhaps I followed too carelessly the Lord's encouragement that we should all "walk with faith" when venturing into the unknown.

Sadly, my head-first encounters with rejection much later in life didn't result in nearly as much compassion as they did in the old days. Even though I probably lost innumerable brain cells in that dark hallway as a child, I'm confident that, as an adolescent, I lost even more at the hands of Hollywood publicists.

One afternoon in early January 1998, my mom noticed me in the family room pacing restlessly. Upon closer inspection, she observed the distressed countenance plastered across my face as I nervously twirled the telephone cord.

"Are you okay?" she asked, unaware that I was being lambasted on the other end of the receiver.

"All I wanted was an interview," I said. "You don't have to threaten me!"

Looking back, this incident was my first real taste of unadulterated rejection. After my third faxed request and fifth or sixth phone inquiry that week, someone finally took my call regarding the star I was trying to book on my fledgling public access show.

"You are the most annoying person I've ever encountered," the woman growled. "My client will *not* be on your show!"

It didn't matter to this unidentified woman that I was just a kid. She just tore into me with reverberating force and hung up before I could even defend my persistence.

Beginning in January 1998, I mailed, faxed, and e-mailed three hundred interview requests to many of the biggest names in the entertainment industry. Every letter was a personalized entreaty garnished with humor and punctuated with the dint of my resolve. Yet, despite the sheer bulk and sincerity of my requests, by early March, every single request had been either flatly declined or conspicuously ignored.

As I recall, many of the excuses were actually quite cordial. Others, however, were altogether devoid of basic human decency. For example:

"We're not taking requests at this time."

"No thank you, but good luck."

"We'll pass."

"My client is currently sick with (insert fabricated illness here)."

"We'll hang on to this request and get back to you at a later time."

"Your parents should have beaten you."

"My client will be out of the country for the next six months."

"If we help you, we will have to help every kid with a talk show."

"You should go after more realistic goals."

"I'm sorry, but I can't help you."

"Thank you so much for contacting us. Please don't contact us again."

"I'll call you right back."

"Don't call us anymore."

"We'll call you if we're interested."

"Do they even have color television in Indiana?"

"Are you mentally challenged or something?"

"I didn't get your request."

"I didn't get your request, but we're still going to pass."

"Did you go to school for bothering people?"

"Perhaps you should get involved with after-school programs."

"Get back to us when you matter."
"No."

Overall, I was rightfully dumbfounded at how vicious and mean-spirited many of these people had shown themselves to be. Strangely enough, though, with time the insults and verbal tirades began wearing less on my nerves. Right from the start, I developed a fairly thick skin that enabled me to persist during the periods where I might have otherwise internally imploded.

One incident in early February, though, almost cracked my rapidly toughening exterior. After several attempts to gain access at a fairly local entertainment venue where several past-their-prime entertainers were scheduled to perform, I finally received backstage clearance from the tour manager of the stage production.

Shortly after the performance, I found myself backstage setting up the video camera on our relatively flimsy tripod. None of the entertainers had stepped off stage yet, so I had a few minutes to breathe calmly before speaking with a celebrity for the first time on camera. Needless to say, the whole experience was incalculably exciting.

But as I stood near the stage exit quietly reviewing the questions on my note cards, one of the venue's employees blindsided me with her presence, which was every bit as wide as her insulting mouth.

Unaware that I had received permission from the tour manager to be backstage, she physically shoved me from behind and knocked me off the top step leading to the stage. I didn't even see it coming. I hit the concrete floor with a thud and then looked up at Satan's little sister.

"You're not supposed to be here," she shouted.

Before I could explain that I had gained access to the facility from the tour manager himself, she had summoned security to escort me from the building.

At this point, my barely controlled excitement had quickly deteriorated into one of the most embarrassing moments of my life. I finally gain access to celebrities and instead of basking in the thrill of my achievement, I get beat up by a girl.

Before I had even gotten off the ground, two security guards had arrived to escort me—a fifteen year old—out of the building. In fact, I wasn't even allowed to grab my own video equipment. The tour manager himself returned my stuff an hour later with sincere apologies. Not surprisingly, I never interviewed a single celebrity for my show that night. But because I didn't want to be seen as a whiny baby who couldn't handle the bumps of the business, I shrugged off the incident and tried to forge ahead.

Making matters difficult, however, were a few unsavory characters from the local media. With the inclusion of my program on the upcoming public access schedule, the local newspapers and radio programs quickly learned of my ambitions.

From being called "a delusional young man with dreams beyond reason" to a "suicide waiting to happen," the general nature of public commentary directed toward my ambition was at first bleak, insulting, and even more embarrassing than getting beaten up by a girl.

When I shared these concerns with Father Stanley one morning after Sunday mass, I was astounded not only by his ability to quickly shrug off such overwhelming rejection and public humiliation but to also rationally analyze my predicament and seemingly make sense of what was really happening.

"Maybe the end result isn't what matters," Father Stanley offered. "Perhaps you're being too selfish. If the career you now choose is really your calling, God surely didn't intend for you to serve a purpose that would only benefit yourself. Maybe you're enduring tribulation because others can learn from how you respond to it."

My competitive mentality at that time would have never—on its own, that is—conceived of any endeavor for which the journey could ultimately mean more than the destination. And although Father Stanley's point was at first exceedingly difficult to accept, he was absolutely correct. In pursuing my dream, I had assumed a great deal of easily overlooked but obviously related responsibility. By aiming so high in life within earshot of thousands of young people through the local media, the eventual outcome of my efforts would serve to either inspire or discourage many in the pursuit of their own dreams—many of which would likely prove ultimately more important than mine.

Determined not to fail myself or anyone to whom I was an underdog role model, I continued with my ambitions and, consequently, the daily grind of rejection. But after a few more months of refusals, insults, and public ridicule, I finally managed to make some headway.

By late spring, I made a substantial contact at the now defunct WB network. At that time Tom Arnold was starring on a sitcom called *The Tom Show*, which only lasted one season.

Auspiciously, I discovered while trying to book Tom Arnold that Ed McMahon was now a recurring character on the same show. Thinking it pointless to get greedy, I temporarily put my request for Mr. Arnold to the wayside and chose to contact the WB publicity department *only* in reference to an interview with Ed McMahon.

Two days after I submitted the request, I received a personal phone call from Ms. Toni Holliday, Ed McMahon's executive assistant.

Seeing "McMahon Communications" flash across the caller ID, I picked up the receiver anticipating yet another quick turn down.

However, Ms. Holliday, a tremendously helpful, gracious woman, proceeded to introduce herself and inform me of the status of my request.

"Well," she said, "Mr. McMahon was pleased to receive your letter."

I almost dropped the phone.

In that instance, I was simply thrilled just to know that Ed McMahon knew I existed!

"Mr. McMahon will be traveling for the next few weeks," she continued, "but he will take you up on your invitation for the live call-in interview on your show. Also, he would be happy to record your opening introduction as requested."

Like a giddy Girl Scout who just sold her first box of cookies, I ardently hopped up and down with joy while maintaining a professional tone that completely belied my uncontrollable elation.

Incredibly, while Ms. Holiday and I were discussing possible dates for the interview, call waiting buzzed in. It was the office of the governor of Indiana! Although I had been trying to get in touch with the governor for months, I didn't click over. Our call waiting button was faulty and I didn't want to risk cutting off Toni for the sake of a likely turndown from the governor. With Mr. McMahon's executive assistant on the line, I could have received a call from the White House and I still wouldn't have risked it.

To be sure, the prospect of publicity was *not* what attracted Ed McMahon to my show. If anybody doesn't need press, it's Ed McMahon. He agreed to appear because he has spent more than a half century of his career helping upcoming talent break into the business—another guardian angel of sorts. And I felt privileged beyond words to sit behind a desk for the first time on my own late night talk and share the moment with this *The Tonight Show* legend.

Ironically, Ed McMahon appeared as the first guest on my show exactly six years to the date—and hour—of the final taping of Johnny Carson's *The Tonight Show*. As always, I made myself available at the guest's convenience. It just happened that Mr. McMahon was free and requested the evening of this particular anniversary.

On the night of the actual taping, I did my best to conceal my nerves and try to present myself as an experienced professional at the ripe old age of fifteen. Although I had only a few weeks to prepare, the moment Ed McMahon joined us on the air there was no turning back.

"My first guest is not only a legend in show business," I began, "he is also a champion of aspiring entertainers and a tireless advocate for numerous charitable causes—including tonight, my show. It gives me great pleasure to welcome an icon of late night talk, Mr. Ed McMahon."

"That was quite an introduction, Michael," Ed chimed in.

"Well," I replied, "I read it just like you wrote it."

That comment generated my first laugh on television.

After our initial exchange of how-do-you-dos, we jumped right into the meat and potatoes of the interview.

During the course of our conversation, McMahon transported my viewers back to his first encounter with the soon-to-be king of late night.

"Johnny Carson was pretty much the same person the day we met in 1958," said McMahon, "as the last day we worked together in 1992."

"He was quiet, very polite, and deeply, deeply private. I think maybe to some extent he might have had a fear of getting too close to people he didn't know very well."

At that moment, I was astonished to learn that Carson and I might have actually shared similar fears at one time in life. Although the curious and excitable kid in me wanted to interject and find out if Johnny had ever thrown up on a casket, I astutely kept to myself and allowed Ed to finish his story uninterrupted.

"The first time we met in New York," Ed continued "Carson had his back turned to me for the entire length of our conversation. I was in his office auditioning for the announcer job on *Who Do You Trust*. And the whole time I was there, Johnny was looking out the window at the Schubert Theatre marquee, which, at that time, was announcing Judy Holliday in *The Bells Are Ringing*."

"Did you even make eye contact?" I asked.

"Only at the very end of our meeting," recalled Mr. McMahon, "when we shook hands. I really thought he didn't like me. But Carson was just very shy."

Undeniably, Ed McMahon provided me with a truly unforgettable and infinitely gracious opportunity to start my broadcasting career with a bang. And as it turned out, all it took was that first interview with Ed to put my show on an absolute roll. Over the next six months, my guest list became a veritable who's who of notables. Within three years, I nabbed interviews with Ray Romano, Kevin Bacon, President Gerald R. Ford, Katie Couric, Walter Cronkite, Leeza Gibbons, and more than one hundred other equally recognized personalities.

Best of all, my local talk show's budding popularity also provoked enormous media attention. From appearances on *The Tonight Show* to numerous profiles in *Time*,

People, and *Entertainment Weekly*, my efforts had now been recognized to a degree that few had ever believed possible. And, true to Father Stanley's conviction, it was the journey to my dream and not the living of it that ultimately proved most meaningful to people.

After five years on local television, *The Michael Essany Show* was picked up by E! Entertainment Television and broadcast nationally for the first time on March 2, 2003. By early April, I had received more than ten thousand pieces of mail from young people my age with similar dreams. Although they didn't all want to be famous television hosts, they all wanted advice. Reminiscent of my letter-writing campaign several years earlier, I was now on the receiving end of the inquiries and certainly more than willing to share my counsel.

In addition to addressing every question posed and offering as much personal wisdom as a young man my age could gather, in every letter I also included an excerpt from one of the most inspiring quotes I had ever read. It was the quote engraved on a plaque I received from the Gerald R. Ford Presidential Museum with congratulatory wishes shortly after my television show went national.

> It is not the critic who counts, nor the man who points out how the strong man stumbled, or where the doer of deeds could have done them better. The credit belongs to the man who is actually in the arena, whose face is marred by dust and sweat and blood; who strives valiantly; who errs and comes short again and again; who knows great enthusiasms, great devotions; who spends himself in a worthy cause; who, at the best, knows in the end the triumph of high achieve-

ment, and who, at the worst, if he fails, at least fails while daring greatly, so that his place shall never be with those timid souls who know neither victory nor defeat.

—Theodore Roosevelt

11

Ambitions and Fears

As one might expect, having a television show does wonders for an individual's social life. Whether it's taken as a perk or a curse is entirely irrelevant. Either way, it's unavoidable. Being on television makes everyone want to be your friend. And although some, if not the majority, are genuine and legitimate, others, to be sure, will not hesitate to use and abuse you in return for something that they want.

By the time I was sixteen years old, the minimal success of my local television show had made me somewhat of a regional celebrity. On the streets, in fact, people would regularly recognize me from television and occasionally ask to attend a show taping. Though, as a young man in my formative—and occasionally awkward—teenage years, I was always most enthralled by the legions of young women who suddenly expressed an interest in me.

Despite my hectic schedule as a busy high school student and even busier television host, I tried to make time for a normal dating life. Even though I habitually failed miserably in this objective, I still gave it a shot. In the end, however, I was far too dedicated to my dream to make a normal teenage relationship work with anyone. Of course, when opportunities presented themselves, past mishaps didn't stop me from trying again.

Shortly before the end of my first season on local television, I met a girl name Julie who lived in Valparaiso. She was familiar with my work and seemed interested in getting to know me better. I invited her to a taping and showed her behind the scenes of my talk show. Although she never seemed too terribly interested in the celebrities that had appeared on the show, one evening over dinner—our first meal together, in fact—she mentioned having seen an advertisement for my upcoming interview with actor Gary Sinise. Best known for his portrayal of Lieutenant Dan in *Forest Gump*, the Oscar-nominated actor was scheduled to appear in Chicago and I snagged an interview with him for my show.

As it turned out, Julie was an enormous fan of Gary Sinise. And over the course of our three weeks of dating, not once did we hang out where she didn't slyly or explicitly inquire about my upcoming interview with Gary. Specifically, she wanted to know when it was scheduled and if she could come along. Although the romantic sentiments of flowers still seemed to resonate with Julie to an extent, it soon became evident that if I could only arrange for Julie to meet Gary Sinise she would probably love me for the rest of my life.

Naturally, I was smitten by this young woman. She was almost two years older than me, smart, funny, and unequivocally drop-dead gorgeous. Growing up, I was always told my maturity far exceeded that of most young men my age. Consequently, it made sense in this regard to date girls who were equally mature. Then again, I was so wrapped up in ambitions and fears beyond my years that I could have easily been dating one of the Golden Girls and still been considered too mature for the relationship.

Because I didn't want the distraction of Julie to take me off my A-game during the interview, I called Gary's publicist prior to our taping to find out if Gary could briefly meet Julie for a photo at his press junket a few days before the scheduled interview. To my giddy astonishment, Sinise and his people granted the request.

I called Julie to tell her the good news.

My girlfriend was so excited she didn't say anything for a number of seconds after I explained what would transpire in only forty-eight hours. After I asked if she was still on the line she screamed and dropped the receiver. For the next minute I overheard Julie excitedly shouting to her mother that she was going to meet Gary Sinise the day after tomorrow. Moments later, Julie returned to the line and thanked me profusely for making her dream come true.

After I gave the instructions on when and where Gary's press junket was taking place, I invited her over for dinner. To my surprise, she declined, citing a lot of homework for school the next day. Either way, she promised to call me tomorrow and once again thanked me for what I had done.

I got off the phone with Julie feeling like an absolute champion. It was no small exaggeration to say that I adored this girl and was thrilled to have made her so perceptibly happy. In that moment, I wholly believed that we had a future together. In fact, she might even be "the one."

The following morning and afternoon I thought about Julie constantly. I couldn't wait for school to let out so that I could talk to her the night before her big meeting with Gary. Strangely, though, by dinnertime I had not yet heard from her. And for the remainder of the evening, my repeated calls went unreturned.

By the following afternoon—roughly two hours after Julie was scheduled to meet Gary—I grew concerned that something terrible might have happened possibly on the drive up to Chicago. I immediately called my contact for

Gary to ask if Julie made it to the press junket. He proceeded to inform me that everything went tremendously well and Julie was "the happiest girl" in all of Chicago.

I never heard from Julie again.

Although it was painful to recognize that I had been used for the sake of my connection to a Hollywood celebrity, I didn't grow bitter or resentful.

As expected, when confronted with unfamiliar emotional turmoil, my fear emerged once more. Because of Julie, I became fearful of others using me just to get what they wanted. I knew my future, no matter how successful, would never be fulfilling without a trusted partner with whom I could share all that fate would have in store for me.

My relationship with Julie made me seriously doubt I would ever find such a partner. In fact, for as long as I had aspired to be in show business, those around me—for one reason or another—often asserted that I would probably end up divorced as a result of my career in the entertainment business.

Understandably, such commentary did not settle well with me. In fact, if there was one aspect of Johnny Carson's life that I didn't seek to emulate, it was his never-ending nuptials. As Bob Newhart once observed, "Johnny's first wife was Joan. His second was Joanne. His third was Joanna. I guess the guy just refuses to spring for new towels."

After Julie vanished, I was reminded by my closest family and friends that I was far too young to worry about serious relationships and marriage anyway. And, although I knew they were right, the little boy within me—the one who once so desperately feared abandonment—had returned to torment my already aching heart.

As hard as I tried to remove the fear of being forever lonely, sometimes it is enormously difficult in the midst of an emotional upheaval to know that everything will indeed be alright. All that I knew for certain at this point was that my relationship with Julie made me extremely cautious of the intentions of those around me. And I was determined to never be caught with my emotional guard down again.

12

The Fighting Spirit

Having met, interviewed or worked with an eclectic array of prominent figures over the previous few years, I was always surprised to learn just how many icons of their respective industries studied anything but their craft in college. Steve Martin, for example, majored in philosophy; Gene Simmons, education; Jodie Foster, literature; Tiger Woods, economics; Conan O'Brien, history; "Weird" Al Yankovic, architecture.

Similarly, it baffled some when I opted not to study television broadcasting. Yet, by the time I started college my intense passion for the television industry had surprisingly grown somewhat diluted. To be sure, I still loved my work, but the exaggerated importance I once attributed to it had waned considerably.

By the time my television series went national, I felt a sense of "mission accomplished" that I never expected to feel so soon in life—especially because I had only achieved a relatively small portion of my overall plan. However, by the start of college, my fervent, almost competitive professional passion had been diverted to a cause that, ironically, my television work had brought me closer to than anything else ever had—my own community.

Throughout my unlikely journey from anonymity to celebrity, the most unexpectedly rewarding aspect of the entire experience was, without question, meeting countless young adults who ultimately discovered their own sense of destiny because they observed me discover mine. Perhaps because I had always concentrated so heavily on the times in life when I felt like a coward, I simply could not recognize that my present success had come as a result of seemingly fearless determination in the face of adversity.

As it turned out, my quest to live a dream profoundly resonated with thousands upon thousands across the country. Ironically, the kid who had once been paralyzed by his own inordinate fears was now internationally recognized for the intrepid pursuit of an improbable dream. As a result, many would soon call upon me to apply that "fighting spirit" to a cause greater than my own professional ambitions.

I didn't realize until my freshman year of college exactly what Father Stanley had meant in early conversation by "life's multiple callings." For as long as I could remember, I assumed that people had one distinct calling that would ultimately summon their unique abilities for the rest of their natural life. But by the time I started to detect a new—or second—calling in my own life, I started reflecting in earnest on more than just Father Stanley's comments on multiple callings. In fact, I also started to make sense of his comments in response to my declared intention to pursue a career in television. "Just know," he said, "that the extraordinary heroes in life are no different from the ordinary in the eyes of God. Just serve him and do his work where it needs to be done."

Never more than today has it been clearer that we inhabit a world recurrently in awe of all the wrong heroes. Amazingly, not until I started becoming well known myself did I recognize that I didn't deserve much of the public adulation I was receiving. Obviously, I wasn't brokering peace between warring nations. If anything, I was just trying to bring a few smiles to my blue-collar viewing audience.

To be fair, of course, there is certainly a long list of notable celebrities who contribute greatly to humanity with their charitable and other philanthropic endeavors. But there still remain those who receive an absolutely inordinate amount of praise—if not worship—in response to doing very little good for anyone but themselves.

In the immediate days that followed the national debut of my show, the relatively mundane calendar that adorned my office wall went from totally barren to completely brimming. Numerous national charitable organizations had contacted me about becoming a spokesman for one program or another. Incredibly, fewer than forty-eight hours after the premiere episode, I had received more than five hundred invitations for speaking engagements. However, because most of the organizations requesting my help were national outfits with a considerable amount of support already—not to mention spokespeople far more recognizable than me—I chose to lend my time to the lower-profile causes: the charitable and nonprofit institutions close to home that are frequently lost amid the giant shadow of national organizations.

From hosting fundraisers for individuals with disabilities to speaking on behalf of concerned citizens at local government meetings, I began investing every minute of my time away from work and college to helping those who needed the fighting spirit they identified in me from television.

In the course of my escalating community involvement, I met countless individuals who have served their hometowns admirably and anonymously, often for longer than three times my own age. Consequently, in very little time at all, I realized that my "celebrated" status as a new television star on the block was utterly meaningless in comparison to the thankless achievements of these ordinary heroes who had quietly but diligently done God's work for most of their adult lives. Time after time, I responded to their life stories and tales of *real* courage in the face of adversity with utter heartfelt astonishment.

As a child, I was well known for my premature concerns about life, death, and my life's ultimate purpose. Barely out of diapers, I was nerve-wracked by fears that rarely settle in before middle age. Similarly, by the time I started college and had become wholly involved in my community, I developed yet another untimely fear. To be sure, it's a concern that weighs upon the shoulders of many at some point during one's later years. Alas, it's the ubiquitous apprehension that arises from questioning if one is really doing all they can to serve God's plan for them. It's a moment when you start asking yourself if you have really found and served your true calling. Have you performed a satisfactory number of good works in the eyes of God? And, if not, what more should you do with what time you have left?

It's quite easy to have a veritable panic attack in response to such questions when you negatively speculate on the answers. Such apprehension comes as a consequence of dwelling in a culture that can't separate the extraordinary heroes from the ordinary ones. That is, we can't all rescue a little old lady from a burning building about to implode. But, on many different occasions, we all have the opportunity to help people in less dramatic ways. And, needless to say, by comparison, it's much easier to forget those less harrowing acts of kindness.

For me, the experience working with community leaders on causes close to my hometown illustrated the growing need for society to stop equating heroism with glory. At some point or another, we've all been heroes—knowingly or not—to someone else. Whether the task is big or small, we all serve God by keeping our eyes open for the instances where we're needed. So even though our greatest humanitarian endeavor may not involve taking a bullet for the President of the United States, most of us have served our community, our country, and our Lord to a greater extent than we will likely ever realize. And although some will forever remain worried that they have not contributed enough to the world around them, my answer to them is the same as it was to myself when I, too, began prematurely doubting my legacy of good works: as long as you can still draw breath, you can still serve God.

While still only a sophomore in college, after my show was sold in syndication overseas and new production had halted, I made a conscious decision to devote more of my time to the largely thankless challenges facing my community. Though I hoped to return again one day to the broadcast medium I loved so dearly, I was presently satisfied, at the very least, knowing that my hard work had inspired scores of young Americans to similarly pursue their purportedly improbable dreams.

Ultimately, my rapidly increasing proclivity for public service rather simplified my eventual declaration of a major. To the dismay of many, I named political science my major with initial minors in economics and history. In addition to the long-term professional benefits of such study, for the short term, my academic emphasis on the social sciences would do the most to help me serve my community, where the political track was always a critical avenue to meaningful change and effectual public service.

Despite what some people believe primarily is encompassed by an education in political science, gifted professors in this field will offer considerably more than textbook explanations of governmental procedure. A skilled instructor will challenge students to link contemporary issues with a historical past. In the process, one learns volumes about historical, sociological, and, of course, political issues spanning a broad expanse of time. And, perhaps most importantly, the clearer one comes to perceive the modern world, the better prepared that individual will be to understand wide-ranging issues across an equally diverse spectrum.

Having been raised in a civically minded family, I was introduced to the importance of public service fairly early in life. Notice, however, that I didn't say I was introduced to the importance of *politics*. I was brought up to believe that there is an inherent difference between public service and politics. Politics just happens to supply one path for performing great works in public service. Most of the time, however, politics is little more than show business for the ugly.

During my first few semesters on the campus of Valparaiso University, the two individuals who did the most to exercise my brain and introduce me to greater ways to serve a great cause were Dr. Larry Baas and Dr. Richard Balkema.

Dr. Baas, chair of the Political Science Department, was my academic advisor throughout college. To this day, Dr. Baas remains one of the most extraordinary individuals I have ever had the privilege of knowing.

As the director of Valparaiso's Community Research and Service Center, Dr. Baas has worked tirelessly to inform community leaders of issues facing the public that require more attentive leadership. Over the course of my college career, Dr. Baas reminded me of the tremendous positive impact even one individual can have on his community when he dedicates his efforts to a worthwhile endeavor.

Like Baas, Dr. Richard Balkema also never failed to ignite my imagination about the potential of community service. But, Dr. Balkema, like few instructors I've ever known, always expressed a genuine, unequivocal faith in today's young generation of Americans—particularly those who will soon lead the nation's industries and bodies of government. He encouraged his students to get involved with public affairs early in life because a "fresh set of eyes" can sometimes help introduce the old guard to new problems they might only perceive once it's too late.

Looking back, the combination of my escalating community entrenchment, the inspiration from brilliant educators, and my own startling realization that some of the greatest works anyone can perform are those in one's own community, I began feeling once more that same unmistakable tugging at my soul that preceded my life's *first* calling. And although I wasn't sure where it would ultimately lead, for one of the first times in my life, I allowed my faith in the future and not my fear of the unknown to direct my subsequent actions. As Father Stanley had advised long ago, "God shows us the way to our duty, even when at first the path is unclear."

13

Taking the Knocks

"A wise old owl sat on an oak; the more he saw the less he spoke; the less he spoke the more he heard; why aren't we like that wise old bird?"

When I first heard this charming quote about the importance of listening, I began reflecting on the vital yet misunderstood role played by the power of observation in detecting God's earthly plans for us. As we've all grudgingly realized by now, God doesn't whisper into our ear succinct instructions for doing his work. Instead, he's imbued us with the ability to observe our surroundings and deduce from opportunities that befall us where we can best serve our purpose.

Although I had lived in Valparaiso for most of my life, it wasn't until I began participating in fundraisers for the Spring Valley Homeless Shelter that I first observed just how significant the homeless problem was in Valparaiso and the surrounding county.

Ironically, around the time of this discovery, I was also introduced to an eye-opening book called *The Working Poor*, in which author David Shipler explores the societal forces subjugating those dwelling in poverty while still working full-time. By dispelling some of the common stereotypes frequently cast upon the homeless, Shipler explains how many become homeless through forces they simply cannot control.

In Valparaiso, among the historical culprits of home-lessness are the lack of affordable housing, outrageous utility costs, and the prevalence of minimum-wage service jobs. It turned out that these escalating factors had been fueling homelessness in and around Valparaiso for decades. As a result, entire families had come to compose the bulk of homeless people in our community.

Over the years, ignoring homelessness didn't make the problem go away. Trusting our elected leaders to remedy the crisis didn't resolve anything either. Spring Valley, on the other hand, had made great strides to combat homelessness and poverty. Needless to say, I was always eager to participate whenever Spring Valley called upon me for assistance with one of its fundraisers.

My favorite event, as I recall, was their much-celebrated annual five-kilometer walk, in which individuals would form their own walking teams and raise big bucks for the shelter.

At one of these walks, despite an otherwise wonderful afternoon, I met a family who kindly shared their poignant story of struggle with me. It was a moving account that served to elevate my composed concern to a level of blistering anger.

This lovely young couple, who had been married for six years, had a baby girl with an uncommon and potentially life-threatening skin condition. Every night at bedtime, she has to be placed in a crib strategically situated beneath a life-saving fluorescent light.

With the wife disabled and the husband laid off work, the family had fallen on substantial economic hard times about six months earlier. Understandably, they also fell behind on their bills.

One night during the dead of winter, their electricity was turned off. For them, covering up with blankets and making do would have been acceptable for the short term. But for their baby girl, dependent on electricity to sustain her critical fluorescent light therapy, the situation quickly amounted to a time-sensitive emergency.

With no family in the general vicinity, they first made repeated calls to the local trustee's office for emergency assistance. A trustee, after all, exists to provide emergency financial aid to local families facing such a menacing crisis.

As it turned out, this loss of power took place on a Thursday evening. Our local trustee of nearly a quarter century, Chuck Conover, who collects what amounts to a full-time government salary of more than $40,000, only holds office hours from Monday through Thursday for three-and-a-half hours each day. If not for a benevolent neighbor taking the baby girl in for the evening, this family would have witnessed their daughter grow seriously ill in a relatively short period of time.

When I first heard this story, I thought I had misunderstood the hours of availability at the trustee's office. But after placing a personal phone call to Mr. Conover the following day, I was astonished to learn that I hadn't misunderstood a word. Despite claims of being available 24/7, the prerecorded answering service provided no emergency telephone number when I called to ask what happens if someone needs help between Thursday afternoon and Monday morning. It was implied that anyone who needs help would simply have to wait until Monday.

As I recall, that walk for Spring Valley, where I first met this inspiring young couple, took place in April 2006. The following month, during the local primary elections, I was beside myself to learn that no challenger had filed to oppose Conover in the general election the following November.

That evening I called a number of my acquaintances in local politics to ask why our trustee was poised to run unopposed for yet another four-year term. "He hasn't been challenged for years," I was told. "His name has been around forever and voters don't even think twice about reelecting him."

The trustee's race was deemed small potatoes in a political season that saw the battle for control of the United States Senate and House of Representatives. But for me, at least, the trustee's race hit much closer to home than most national political issues. And I believed it warranted immediate attention.

Despite being only twenty-three-years-old at the time, on June 21, 2006, I announced my candidacy for trustee in the November 7 General Election.

Although I was young, I had already spent a good number of years advocating to young people in classrooms, older folks at Rotary meetings, and audiences of all ages in between, that when individuals are roused to a call for service, they are obligated by their own morality to answer. I would have been a spineless hypocrite—in my own eyes if not anyone else's—if I had allowed the incumbent to run unopposed yet again. I felt passionately about the issues at stake and, despite the fear of running for office with such odds stacked against me, there were no other factors to consider. I knew I had to do this.

Luckily, I beat the filing deadline for candidate vacancies on the Porter County general election ballot by only a few days. I now had a lock on the nomination. And with little more than four months before the polls opened, I had to mount my first political campaign from scratch and oppose a man who had been in office for as long as I had been alive.

One week after I declared my candidacy, an unscientific online poll showed that if the election were held the following day, I would have lost—badly. The poll showed me losing by more than 87 percent of the vote. Further complicating the political landscape was the last minute declaration of a third-party candidate. It was now a three-way battle with Conover seeming the apparent landslide victor.

In Valparaiso, the voting public is an intelligent, nononsense group of citizens completely unimpressed by so-called celebrity status. For the most part, people just didn't perceive a problem in the trustee's office. So no matter who was more popular—me or the incumbent—people were going to cast their votes on the basis of what they perceived. And although I respected this quality in voters, I also remained confident that the 87 percent who continued to blindly entrust their faith in Mr. Conover had seriously misjudged their evaluation of our longtime trustee's job performance.

Beginning shortly after the Fourth of July weekend in the summer of 2006, my campaign began in earnest. It also began, ironically enough, in absolute poverty. Because I vowed to run my campaign without holding a single fundraiser, I planned instead to go door to door and personally speak to every voter who would actually take the time to listen. So while Mr. Conover's campaign spent large sums of money on television ads, direct mail, yard signs, billboards, T-shirts, and newspaper ads, I stuck to my guns and took my message directly to the people.

Incredibly, after only three months of campaigning on foot, the latest poll now showed me with better than 45 percent of public support. Although the polls still put me behind the incumbent by a few percentage points, I was thrilled beyond words knowing that more people than ever in Valparaiso were becoming aware of the pressing issues of homelessness, poverty, and the perceived lack of compassion in the trustee's office.

Heading into the homestretch of the campaign the trustee's race was dubbed by local pundits as highly "playable." Of course, all along I was in it to win. But only in the final two weeks of the campaign did others finally begin to recognize that I had a shot.

Naturally, though, the better I performed in the polls, the harder I was hit by my critics. And in the final days of the campaign, the public was barraged by literature implying that I was far too young and inexperienced to serve as township trustee.

On election night, a number of local candidates—including me—gathered at Casa Del Roma, a charming little banquet hall near downtown Valparaiso. Those in attendance nervously meandered throughout the room, while a jumbo display sat poised to reveal the election returns as they came in. For everyone on the ballot that evening, it was a nerve-wracking wait between the time the polls closed at 6 o'clock and the first posting of returns around seven-thirty. Unfortunately, the first numbers roughly placed me at 47 percent in the three-way race, just six hundred votes out of the lead. Unfortunately, for the next two hours very little changed with regard to those numbers. And by ten o'clock on election night, I placed second in the three-way race and conceded the election to the six-term incumbent.

Surprisingly, amid the morose environment of my first political defeat, I didn't feel anything like a failure. Although we often fear the prospect of failure and, subsequently, never pursue our heartfelt endeavors, from the ashes of my defeat arose the realization that the cause I championed had succeeded in raising the level of public debate in my community.

In this regard, sometimes a defeat is just as significant as a victory if the points made serve to inspire elected officials to be more diligent in confronting issues that had been ignored for far too long.

Without question, my failed bid for the trustee's office succeeded not only in bringing the community's poverty issues further to light, it also relegated another one of my long-held fears to the trash bin of conquered emotional struggles. No longer was failure an impetus for fear in my life.

Some have observed that it's virtually impossible to deduce from the teachings of Christ that God wants his children to forever remain comfortably inside their life's little comfort zones. Instead, God has imbued each of us with an intrinsic courage—whether we realize it or not—to fight the battles that we think we cannot win but that he needs us to fight.

In this regard, there is no such thing as a categorical failure. Instead, there is only feedback. In other words, God wants us to look at our disappointments not as failures, but as the results of an endeavor. And from these results come not only lessons about how we can serve as productive individuals in the years to follow, but illustrations of—if we look hard enough—the positive impact that our perceived failures have actually had on our communities and on our own lives.

Unless we embrace the prospect of failure as merely one integral and rewarding step toward complete success, we will never serve our individual purpose to a full capacity. And, for me, all it took was getting knocked down in an election to make me never again fearful of getting knocked down in life.

14

The Shared Spirit

As I watched my belongings slowly traverse through the colossal X-ray machine at the first security checkpoint, I found myself eagerly anticipating what was poised to be among the most exciting, inspiring, and ultimately patriotic experiences of my life.

Shortly before two o'clock, I was ushered through the northwest gate of the White House and escorted to the lobby of the West Wing. On this truly remarkable occasion, I was fortunate to be included among the small number of attendees at a ceremony scheduled to take place in the famed East Room.

Soon after the group of fewer than two hundred dignitaries was asked to be seated quietly, the president of the United States was introduced to our presence and given a rousing ovation. But before the commander in chief had even entered my line of sight, I realized that this extraordinary occasion was exactly what I would have earmarked several years earlier as an experience I would never have wanted to share alone and without my life's partner.

As the president made his brief march to the podium with Miss USA Rachel Smith at his side, I similarly looked to my side and took the hand of another beauty in attendance. It was the hand of my wife, Christa, whom I had married only a few days earlier.

In Washington, DC, for a truly unforgettable honeymoon, Christa and I had first met four years earlier while both students at Valparaiso University. Quite literally the answer to my prayers, Christa was an absolute blessing in my life. In addition to being a trusted partner, a close friend, and an unequaled confidante, Christa represented the very antithesis of what I had first come to fear in the wake of my relationship with Julie. In fact, when Christa and I first met, she was among only a few girls in college who didn't know—or care—that I was on television. Ultimately, Christa loved me for me, just as I loved her for her.

In what surely amounted to be the newlywed experience of a lifetime, Christa and I visited the Oval Office, crossed paths with the secretary of state, posed for photographs in the Rose Garden, marveled at the Center and Cross Halls of the main foyer, toured the West Wing, and attended a private function with the president of the United States.

Yet, despite the sheer magnificence of the White House and our noble company, nothing inspired more awe in my heart than knowing that I had found a partner like Christa with whom I could share the rest of my life. In no uncertain terms, her presence removed many of my deepest fears about trust, partnership, and true love.

Ever since I was kid, I lived what can best be described as "an accelerated existence." That is, my ambitions, maturity, and fears were always advanced far beyond my physical age. As a result, it often seemed that I was living life in fast-forward, never quite able to slow down, relax, and enjoy the majesty and serenity of the peaceful world that dwelled just beyond the frantic little bubble of my own existence. With Christa by my side, however, I was perfectly content for the first time in my life with the moment I presently knew.

Surprisingly, my relationship with Christa never gave rise to any subsequent fears about the prospect of divorce. As someone who often dwells on numbers or statistical evidence before making an important decision, I was well aware of the divorce rates among couples in our age group. Nonetheless, for one of the first times in my life, I didn't worry about what the compelling evidence ominously suggested. Even though half of all couples divorce, I believe the adage that couples who pray together stay together. Perhaps even more important than our love for one another, Christa and I share a deep faith together. And in that faith we absorb each other's fears and share each other's hopes as we proceed through life as stronger individuals because of our united spirit in God's love.

Throughout their forty-eight years of marriage, my grandparents illustrated the positive effect God exerts on a marriage when couples unite in their faith and make God an equal partner in marriage. Growing up, in fact, I often admired the engraved sterling-silver wall plate that adorned my grandparents' small bedroom. It was a simple prayer that not only spoke to the immense strength of Grandma's and Grandpa's indistinguishable romance, it also revealed the source.

Lord Jesus,
Grant that I and my spouse may have a true and
    understanding love for each other.
Grant that we may both be filled with faith and trust.
Give us the grace to live with each other in peace and
    harmony.
May we always bear with one another's weaknesses
    and grow from each other's strengths.

Help us to forgive one another's failings, and grant us
    patience, kindness, cheerfulness, and the spirit of
    placing the well-being of one another ahead of self.
May the love that brought us together grow and
    mature with each passing year.
Bring us both ever closer to you through our love for
    each other.
Let our love grow to perfection.
Amen.

Long before even high school dating was on my radar,
my grandfather told me that for love to endure, it must
evolve beyond the heady romantic affection that insubstan-
tially provides the foundation for many short-term mar-
riages. In fact, even in childhood I could already see the
mature love rooted in the faith my grandparents shared.

From praying with one another to remaining actively
involved in their church, my grandparents' faith was proac-
tive, secure, and a consistent part of their daily lives.

When Christa and I were first married, we began similar traditions to those practiced by my grandparents. For
us, involving God in our marriage meant a great deal more
than just sharing a religious denomination and attending
church. Today we share our faith as much as we share our
future.

And apart from my fear that her cat will never love me
as much as he loves her, there are very few apprehensions
that married life has bestowed upon me so far—a very good
sign, indeed.

15

The Top Ten Lessons

For several years now I have been traveling what some have called "The Mashed Potato Circuit." After graduating college, syndicating my show overseas, and embarking on a number of rewarding publishing ventures, my life suddenly acquired the newfound luxury of time. As a result, I began accepting invitations for speaking engagements, commencement addresses, and motivational talks. In other words, I have spent a considerable amount of time on the road. But no matter where the travels take me, there's always one question people ask: "What makes you so fearless?"

If only they knew.

As a little boy, I feared that which I didn't understand. As an adolescent, I feared that which I couldn't control. Today, as an adult, I only fear waking up and realizing that my tremendous odyssey of personal growth and renewed faith was but a dream.

From throwing up on Aunt Lucille's casket to now starting a family of my own, life has taken me a long way. My faith, however, has taken me even further. But what mostly separates the *new* me from the *old* me is the valuable experience I gained from years of brutal hand-to-hand combat with fear itself. And as I reflect on the many lessons learned through my journey from living life in fear to ultimately welcoming it with faith, I am left with ten vital lessons that continue guiding me today.

1. Expect More...and Less

On many occasions growing up, I would have likely felt God's comforting presence only if he had personally called collect to tell me that I wasn't forgotten.

The incredible paradox of our faith is that we either expect far too much or far too little from it. Throughout much of my life, for example, I passionately sought irrefutable evidence that God walked beside me in times of doubt and despair. With time and maturity, I was able to reflect on the ways in which he had been there for me, despite my inability to perceive it at the time. Yet, when I didn't see or feel all that I wished to see or feel in those difficult moments, I grew doubtful. And, time and time again, I allowed my own misguided expectations to dictate the strength of my faith in God's unfailingly watchful presence.

> On that day, when evening had come, he said to them, "Let us go across to the other side." And leaving the crowd, they took him with them in the boat, just as he was. And other boats were with him. And a great storm of wind arose, and the waves beat into the boat, so that the boat was already filling. But he was in the stern, asleep on the cushion; and they woke him and said to him, "Teacher, do you not care if we perish?" And he awoke and rebuked the wind, and said to the sea, "Peace! Be still!" And the wind ceased, and there was a great calm. He said to them, "Why are you afraid? Have you no faith?" —Mark 4:35–40

Similarly, there were just as many occasions growing up when I expected considerably less from my faith than I rightly should have. Initially, I possessed an erroneous confidence that God was supposed to do all the heavy lifting for me when confronted by one of life's many challenges. Once I caught on to the reality that he wasn't going to do that for me, it became much easier to accept my fear than my faith. Sadly, it took many years before I realized that the challenges that lie before us in this lifetime are not the *real* challenges. The real challenge is dictated from above. It is a challenge to our faith—our faith in God and our faith in ourselves to do what we must in order to serve our purpose— grand or miniscule. And in this endeavor, our faith is absolutely imperative. It is also sufficient to see us through any impediment. As Mother Teresa once observed, "I know God will not give me anything I can't handle. I just wish he didn't trust me so much."

2. Talk to God

My father used to joke that there was a time when he couldn't wait until I spoke my first words. Then, once I started speaking, he couldn't wait for me to shut up.

In retrospect, I was an exceedingly talkative youngster. But while I had no difficulty whatsoever opening up to those around me, I could not communicate so openly with God. With time, I realized that I was not alone in this exceedingly difficult objective. In other words, we all pray to God. Few of us, however, actually *talk* to Him.

As I grew older, it became clear that my initial reluctance to engage in conversation with God was based in part on my somewhat limited definition of "conversation." Most define a conversation as a verbal exchange between or among individuals in which everyone speaks in turn. Growing up, I found talking to God largely pointless because he would not respond, at least not according to standard conversation etiquette.

It was not until I began openly speaking to God—aloud at times—either in church or the privacy of my own bedroom that I realized that God responds to conversation, not with an audible reply from a booming voice above, but in the peace and quiet of the heart. As Father Stanley once told me, God speaks to us through our emotions and feelings. This is why many people, I've learned, keep a pad and paper at their nightstand. Before bed, after praying to God, one can easily find oneself imbued with a rush of thoughts or emotions. When the pen is put to paper, such feelings emerge as ideas, messages, or encouragements. A person of faith will realize that these communications are God responding to the conversations we initiate.

In times of doubt, we must recall how God communicated with Peter as he prayed upon the roof in Joppa. We must recall how God communicated to Paul and inspired his apostolic ministry. Like Elijah, we must recall that God speaks to us within our hearts, not only in the eternal realm of our earthly senses.

> And behold, the LORD passed by, and a great and strong wind tore into the mountains and broke the rocks in pieces before the LORD, but the LORD was not in the wind; and after the wind an earthquake, but the LORD was not in the earthquake; and after the earthquake a fire, but the LORD was not in the fire; and after the fire a still small voice.—1 Kings 19:11–12

Whether we realize it or not, God's spirit dwells inside of us. And through a variety of ways, God communicates with us through that spirit. For those ravaged by fear and doubt, nothing can so quickly calm such anxieties as engaging in conversation with him who can just as easily calm the seas.

3. Worship with Faith

There is no shortage of people in this world who fear God to a baseless, illogical, and completely unhealthy extent. For these misinformed individuals, God does not exist primarily as the Creator of heaven and earth, the Giver of life, and the source of all beauty, love, and forgiveness in our majestic world. Instead, he is seen almost exclusively as the supreme and severe punisher of those who fail to flawlessly serve his will.

As a child, I was nerve-wracked by the possibility of displeasing God and being sentenced to dwell forever with my buddy Paul in the spaghetti-free environment that is eternal damnation. At the time I thought God wanted everyone to cower in terror from the prospect of being separated from his love. What I was choosing to ignore were the many times God had said "fear not," "be not afraid," or "have no fear." Indeed, fear is not something the Lord wishes us to possess, let alone use as the foundation for our faith.

In most cases, excluding those who would flagrantly disregard his word and impugn his teachings, the fear described in the Bible has little or no connection to fear in the sense of hellfire and brimstone. The "fear of God" is intended to convey a reverence for his awesome power. Repeatedly, in fact, the Bible suggests that God wants us to serve him and one another, not because we fear the consequences of doing otherwise, but because it is right and just to do so. Similarly, we should fear separation from God, not because he shall punish us otherwise, but because we will suffer in the absence of his life-sustaining love.

Few things are as cumbersome as proceeding through life beneath the enormous weight of intense fear. For many of us, the fear of not being "good enough" in the eyes of God is the widespread cause of many common anxieties. As someone who once bore the burden of similar thinking, I failed to identify that the very existence of my concern for displeasing God confirms my secure relationship with him. And those who are secure in their relationship with God certainly have no logical reason to live in fear of him.

> There is no fear in love; but perfect love casteth out fear: because fear hath torment. He that feareth is not made perfect in love.—1 John 4:18

4. Recognize Your Purpose

Before I had even lost my final baby tooth, I had begun wondering as to the ultimate purpose of my life. In my mind, there was no acceptable wiggle room for uncertainty. I wanted to know. Come to think of it, I *needed* to know.

Similar to my exaggerated worry, a recurring source of great fear for many is the concern born of never finding and serving one's true purpose. For some, this fear arises early; for others, much later. But, eventually, we all wonder why we were put here and if we're really serving our intended calling.

For this reason, realizing one's exact purpose in life is ultimately less important than realizing that one's life *has* purpose. Whether you discover it early or late in life—if ever—is actually irrelevant, especially to God.

For I know the plans I have for you, plans to bring you prosperity and not to harm you, plans to give you hope and a future.—Jeremiah 29:11

Those who repeatedly ask God if they should really be where they are today lack faith in knowing that God guides everyone to exactly where they are supposed to be. If we are open and receptive to his signs and influences, we will ultimately find our path and, consequently, serve his will, which is our purpose. But as I discovered through my youthful ambitions, we can only remove our fear of not serving a great purpose by first coming to terms with what a great purpose truly is.

As we've discussed, each of God's individual children is called to serve him and one another in a uniquely individual way. While some perform years of missionary work in foreign lands, others perform seemingly more ordinary good works closer to home. Both contributions, however, are recognized equally in the eyes of the Lord. After all, if everyone was called to missionary work, there would be no one left to attend to the myriad of other good works God needs us to perform.

For this reason, we must always trust that we are in life exactly where God wants us—and needs us—to be. Anyone who claims a secure relationship with God must believe that God is entrusting them to do what they were called to do—whether it's obvious or obscure.

5. The Valleys Foreshadow the Peaks

Because of the accepted role that fear plays in life, it is almost impossible at times to comprehend how anything "bad" may, in the long run, actually be for "our own good."

But, as my personal experiences illustrate, one simply cannot understand or appreciate the highest peak without first learning the valuable lessons indigenous to the deepest valleys.

> Though he fall, he shall not be utterly cast down:
> for the LORD upholdeth him with his hand.
> —Psalm 37:24

Often in life we spend—or, more accurately, waste—a great deal of time fearing potential outcomes that we can't possibly influence or control. My experience has led me to a considerably more practical use of my innate proclivity for apprehension. Realizing that things are not always going to go our way and that heartache, at times, is inevitable, it is far more important that we learn from disappointments rather than avoid them altogether. God, after all, has been known to employ a wide variety of communication methods to teach us a lesson or prove an invaluable point.

When a series of mishaps befalls one, it is remarkably easy to grow fearful of an endless continuation of the status quo. In truth, however, there is absolutely nothing to fear from enduring the valleys that always manage to precede the attainment of a desired peak. It's a process that begins by trusting God and his plan for each of us.

6. Failure Is Neither Final Nor Fruitless

Prior to embarking on the quest to live my dream and hopefully serve a worthwhile purpose, I had always thought of success and failure to be mutually exclusive, with the former naturally more desirable than the latter. My experiences both in victory and defeat ultimately proved that neither is the leading gauge of accomplishment.

> Likewise, exhort the young men to be sober-minded, in all things showing yourself to be a pattern of good works; in doctrine showing integrity, reverence, incorruptibility, sound speech that cannot be condemned, that one who is an opponent may be ashamed, having nothing evil to say of you.—Titus 2:6–8

Throughout the Bible, numerous passages address the importance of leading by sound example, not through concrete failure or success. Prior to Father Stanley's consultation about the journey of an endeavor meaning more than its completion, I had always feared the prospect of failure. Apart from the sheer embarrassment of appearing a loser to those you respect, failure seems to foreshadow a life devoid of the sacred hopes you wish to be realized. Given the lengths to which many will go—in politics or sports, for example—to avoid defeat, it is apparent that societal standards regard failure as a grotesque mark of shame and humiliation to be avoided at almost any conceivable cost. As a result, the fear of failure precludes many from even attempting to achieve, no matter how grand or insignificant the objective.

The eventual dissolution of my fear of failure was born of the understanding that failure is only absolute if no examples were set during the journey. Yet, if another individual—either presently or in the future—can learn anything at all from your conduct of character during the endeavor in question, there is nothing about that failure that is fruitless or final. Examples indeed live longer than victories, both in the subsequent conduct by witnesses to the example and in the memories of those personally touched by the example.

7. Trust Your Inner Strength

Throughout much of my childhood and adolescence, there were few things of which I was more frightened than myself. From worrying that I was not a good enough person to fearing that I might never realize my dreams, I routinely was fraught by concerns born of my perceived ability to do this or that.

Without question, many of our deepest fears in life are related to our own self-doubts; our inability in times of uncertainty, struggle, or indecision to believe that we have the wisdom and courage to do what we must. As a result, the shelves of most contemporary bookstores are replete with self-help guides for the millions of poor souls subjugated by their own self-doubt.

Perhaps a considerable amount of shelf space would become newly available if we could only remind ourselves more frequently that we are all made in his likeness. In other words, we are all extensions of God. And, if overcoming many of our greatest fears begins with simply having more faith in God, similarly, we must also work to welcome a greater faith in ourselves—not because a self-help guru suggested so, but because the power of God rests within us to conquer any earthly challenge.

The Bible teaches us that God has bestowed upon humanity what is universally recognized as free will, which likewise reflects God's image. That is, like God, we think, decide, and experience a variety of emotions. In light of this gift, God has enabled every individual to direct his or her own actions. Contrary to what some believe, those with faith in God do not follow their chosen course alone.

> I can do all things through Him who strengthens me. —Philippians 4:13

The process of renewing our faith in ourselves begins with understanding that we simply cannot doubt ourselves without also doubting the strength, courage, and wisdom that God has placed in us to reflect his unfaltering presence in our lives.

8. Dwell Less on the Moment

When something bad happens, the moment in which the negative event transpires always amplifies to an exaggerated extent the severity of the entire situation and its ramifications.

Growing up, I regularly found myself paralyzed in the moment when something terrible had first occurred. Whether it was the sickness of a loved one or the unintended consequence of a foolish personal decision, I always dwelled so heavily on the moment that my inability to find faith in those instances was only further complicated.

> In time of trouble…He shall set me upon a rock.
> —Psalms 27:5

With time and perspective, I can now reflect with a smile on numerous occasions that, at least at the time, appeared to foreshadow the end of the world as I practically knew it. As it was, many of my fears were allowed to take root in the feelings of despair that unfailingly accompanied such undesirable situations. Unfortunately, as a youngster I was not able to perceive the multitude of ways in which I was both blowing the situation out of proportion and failing to detect the many ways that things could have been worse if not for God's unyielding watchfulness over me.

In times of trouble, we are notorious for needlessly dwelling on our worst fears rather than our best hopes. But no matter the situation, things are never as bad as they initially seem. Had I replaced my panic with prayer in times of trouble setting in, I would have more rapidly found peace in knowing that all would be resolved in due time through the unrivaled power and unequalled love of God.

9. The Unknown Is Known

As intellectual beings with instinctual curiosity, few things in life are as difficult for our rational minds to accept as the unknown. During childhood, my deepest fears were consistently rooted in the unanswerable questions that routinely sprung from my curious brow. It was not until I began to grow in my faith did I realize that when we fully surrender ourselves to God, we become instruments of his wisdom.

What is unknown to us is not unknown to him. Consequently, the closer we are to God, the closer we are to finding comfort in our lives overflowing with unknowns.

> He is the unveiler of deep and secret things: he has knowledge of what is in the dark, and the light has its living-place with him. —Daniel 2:22

10. Embrace Your Fear

While it may seem utterly incongruous to do so now, there can truly be no honest discussion about fear without acknowledging why, in the final analysis, we should all embrace it.

Indeed, for as long as we dwell in human form, fear will remain an integral and irremovable part of our existence. For me, fear played a huge role throughout my life. Yet rather than believing that I ultimately succeeded in spite of my fears, I have come to the realization that I might have succeeded largely because of them.

Although fear cannot be fully erased, it can certainly be controlled. When we harness the power of our fear and enable it to inspire us rather than consume us, fear can do many things to our benefit. It can kick start our faith. It can keep us alert and at the peak of performance. And, for all its negative implications, fear can be one of the greatest driving forces for personal, professional, and spiritual growth available to us.

As a little boy, I perpetually looked up to those around me who appeared to have greater courage and strength than I could ever hope to have. What I didn't realize at the time was that God packs each of our spiritual suitcases with the same essentials. No individual at birth is better equipped to control or resist fear than another individual. But, over time, we each learn to overcome our fears according to the effort we muster and the faith we summon.

> Have I not commanded you? Be strong and courageous. Do not be terrified; do not be discouraged, for the LORD your God will be with you wherever you go.—Joshua 1:9

96

When viewed as a great impetus for action and service, fear may very well be among God's greatest blessings to all of humanity. For in the final analysis it is fear that so often motivates our faith, mobilizes our efforts, and renews our trust in God to see us through the darkness of night and always deliver us to a brighter tomorrow.

16

Enjoying the Spaghetti

Three weeks before the culmination of my childhood dream to appear on *The Tonight Show*, the man who had so richly instilled in me as much humor as he did faith, Father Stanley Milewski, passed away at the age of eighty-four.

Although I was unable to share with Father Stanley the subsequent achievements and milestones in my life, even after he departed his earthly family, Father Stanley continued giving of his enormous faith to those he loved.

Shortly following Father Stanley's passing, I received a small collection of his prayers that would beautifully supplement my own collection of prayers most relevant and meaningful in my life.

Without Father Stanley, the love of my closest family and friends, the power of my faith, and the love of God, I would have never survived the battlefield of fear that was once my own mind. As Winston Churchill famously observed, kites rise highest against the wind, not with it. In this regard, a kite is a particularly appropriate analogy for the human spirit. Fear is always the precursor to faith's finest hour. Indeed, there remains no quick fix, no antidote, no medicinal substance, and certainly no self-help guide that can ultimately achieve what only he can through your faith in him.

I only hope that my personal transition from a life lived in fear to one treasured in faith can somehow provide a source of inspiration to those presently ravaged by that which my faith helped me to overcome.

It was a process that began with prayer and—fittingly—should conclude with the same.

A Prayer for Courage

Holy Father,
I pray for courage as I begin this day,
for I understand there is work to be done, burdens to
    be carried, feelings to be shared, and joys to be
    celebrated.
Grant me the courage to be silent that I may hear
    Thy voice;
to persevere, that I may share Thy victory; and to
    remember,
lest I forget the way by which Thou has led me.
And when this day is done, O Lord, may I have the
    courage to see Thy guiding hand in the friendships
    that have been made, in the hurts that have been
    healed, and in the strength that has been given.
Amen.